Facilitating Evidence-Based Practice for Students with ASD
A Classroom Observation Tool for Building Quality Education

by

Christina R. Carnahan, Ed.D.
University of Cincinnati
Ohio

and

K. Alisa Lowrey, Ph.D.
University of Southern Mississippi
Hattiesburg

with invited contributors

Baltimore • London • Sydney

Paul H. Brookes Publishing Co.
Post Office Box 10624
Baltimore, Maryland 21285-0624
USA
www.brookespublishing.com

Copyright © 2018 by Paul H. Brookes Publishing Co., Inc.
All rights reserved.

"Paul H. Brookes Publishing Co." is a registered trademark of
Paul H. Brookes Publishing Co., Inc.

Typeset by BMWW, Windsor Mill, Maryland.
Manufactured in the United States of America by Sheridan Books, Inc., Chelsea, Michigan.

All examples in this book are composites. Any similarity to actual individuals or circumstances is coincidental, and no implications should be inferred.

Purchasers of *Facilitating Evidence-Based Practice for Students with ASD* are granted permission to download, print, and photocopy the blank forms in the text for educational purposes. These forms may not be reproduced to generate revenue for any program or individual. Photocopies may only be made from an original book. *Unauthorized use beyond this privilege may be prosecutable under federal law.* You will see the copyright protection notice at the bottom of each photocopiable page.

Cover image is © istock/gradyreese.

Library of Congress Cataloging-in-Publication Data

Names: Carnahan, Christina, author. | Lowrey, K. Alisa, author.
Title: Facilitating evidence-based practice for students with ASD : a classroom observation tool for
    building quality education / Christina R. Carnahan and K. Alisa Lowrey ; with invited contributors.
Description: Baltimore, Maryland : Paul H. Brookes Publishing Co., 2018. |
    Includes bibliographical references and index.
Identifiers: LCCN 2018005329 (print) | LCCN 2018019938 (ebook) |
    ISBN 9781681253015 (epub) | ISBN 9781681253022 (pdf) | ISBN 9781598579413 (paperback)
Subjects: LCSH: Autistic children—Education. | Observation (Educational method) |
    BISAC: EDUCATION / Special Education / General. | EDUCATION / Special Education /
    Mental Disabilities. | EDUCATION / Classroom Management.
Classification: LCC LC4717 (ebook) | LCC LC4717 .C367 2018 (print) | DDC 371.94—dc23
LC record available at https://lccn.loc.gov/2018005329

British Library Cataloguing in Publication data are available from the British Library.

2022   2021   2020   2019   2018

10   9   8   7   6   5   4   3   2   1

Table of Contents

About the Downloads..v
About the Authors vii
About the Contributors... ix
Foreword   *Brooke Carson*.. xi
Foreword   *Kevin Ayres* xii
Preface...xv
Acknowledgments... xvii
Introduction xix

1   Understanding the Learning and Behavioral Needs of Students With ASD 1
    Christina R. Carnahan, Kate Doyle, and K. Alisa Lowrey

2   Laws Every Leader Needs to Know: A Look at Legislation, Regulations, Case Law,
    and Individuals With ASD..15
    K. Alisa Lowrey, Mitchell L. Yell, and Gregory W. Smith

3   Evidence-Based Practices for Students With ASD: How Will I Know It When
    I See It?...29
    K. Alisa Lowrey and Christina R. Carnahan

4. The Evidence-Based Classroom Observation Tool for Creating Building-
    and District-Level Capacity 39
    Christina R. Carnahan, K. Alisa Lowrey, and Kate Snyder

5   Developing and Leading Collaborative School Cultures..71
    Pamela Williamson, Christina R. Carnahan, and Sarah J. Letson

Appendix   Development of a Standardized Benchmark Assessment Tool to
           Facilitate EBP for Students With ASD...83

Glossary...99
References 105
Index 113

About the Downloads

Purchasers of this book may download, print, and/or photocopy the blank forms for educational use. These materials are included with the print book and are also available at **www.brookespublishing.com/carnahan** for both print and e-book buyers.

About the Authors

Christina R. Carnahan, Ed.D., University of Cincinnati, Ohio
Christina R. Carnahan is an associate professor of special education within the School of Education in the College of Education, Criminal Justice, and Human Services at the University of Cincinnati, where she teaches undergraduate and graduate courses in the field of moderate to intense disabilities. She is also the director of Advancement and Transition Services (http://cech.uc.edu/education/ats.html) within the School of Education. Dr. Carnahan's research interests include building communication and literacy for individuals with autism spectrum disorder and developmental disabilities and creating efficient and effective instruction and support practices across the life span. Dr. Carnahan has published in journals such as *Exceptional Children, Journal of Special Education,* and *Focus on Autism and Developmental Disabilities.*

K. Alisa Lowrey, Ph.D., University of Southern Mississippi
K. Alisa Lowrey is an associate professor of special education within the Department of Curriculum, Instruction, and Special Education in the College of Education and Psychology at the University of Southern Mississippi (USM), where she teaches undergraduate and graduate courses in the field of special education. Dr. Lowrey is the coeditor for *Focus on Autism and Other Developmental Disabilities.* Her research interests include inclusive practices, universal design for learning, and quality teacher preparation and professional development, specifically focusing on those learners with the most significant support needs. Dr. Lowrey has published in journals such as *Research and Practice for Persons with Severe Disabilities, Intellectual and Developmental Disabilities,* and *Education and Training in Autism and Developmental Disabilities.*

About the Contributors

Shawn K. Bishop, M.S., BCBA, Michigan State University, East Lansing, MI
Shawn K. Bishop is a board-certified behavior analyst who graduated with a master's degree in psychology from the Applied Behavior Analysis program at the University of Southern Mississippi. She currently works as a behavior analyst at The Early Learning Institute for Michigan State University. The Early Learning Institute specializes in early intensive behavioral interventions for young learners with autism spectrum disorder.

Kate Doyle, Ph.D., Mount St. Joseph University, Cincinnati, OH
Kate Doyle obtained her doctoral degree from the University of Cincinnati. She is currently an assistant professor and director of the Special Education program at Mount St. Joseph University. Kate serves as an educational consultant to many greater Cincinnati schools. Her research interests include social skills interventions, language and literacy instructional strategies, and behavioral interventions for individuals with low-incidence disabilities.

Jobina Khoo, M.A., Northwestern State University of Louisiana, Natchitoches, LA
Jobina Khoo, a doctoral candidate in Research, Evaluation, Statistics, and Assessment (RESA) at the University of Southern Mississippi, worked as a production editorial assistant for Dr. K. Alisa Lowrey, who is the coeditor of *Focus on Autism and Other Developmental Disabilities*. Khoo is an assistant professor in the Department of Health and Human Performance at Northwestern State University of Louisiana.

Sarah J. Letson, M.A., University of North Carolina at Greensboro, Greensboro, NC
Sarah Letson is a doctoral student in the Specialized Education Services department at the University of North Carolina at Greensboro. She is also studying cognitive neuroscience at Duke University. Ms. Letson's research interests include reading comprehension, motivation, and the use of evidence-based practices for students with learning disabilities and autism spectrum disorder.

Gregory W. Smith, Ph.D., University of Southern Mississippi, Hattiesburg, MS
Gregory Smith is an assistant professor in the Department of Curriculum, Instruction, and Special Education at the University of Southern Mississippi. Dr. Smith's research interests include high-incidence disabilities, cognition, and memory.

Kate Snyder, Ed.D., Novia Scotia Community College, Halifax, Nova Scotia
Dr. Kate Snyder is a special advisor, teaching and learning, at the Nova Scotia Community College. She is an educator who has taught in both general and special education in K–12 settings as well as in postsecondary teacher education programs. Dr. Snyder is committed to collaborating with students and colleagues to design accessible learning environments and to promote educational practices that engage all learners.

Pamela Williamson, Ph.D., University of North Carolina at Greensboro, Greensboro, NC
Pamela Williamson is an associate professor at the University of North Carolina at Greensboro. She has experience working with individuals with autism spectrum disorder and their teachers in reading intervention and instruction. She has published numerous peer-reviewed articles related to reading and autism spectrum disorder in journals such as *Exceptional Children* and *Teaching Exceptional Children*. In addition, she is the coeditor of an award-winning textbook, *Quality Literacy Instruction for Students with Autism Spectrum Disorders,* and has educated in-service educators, related services personnel, and families on this topic across the United States.

Mitchell L. Yell, Ph.D., University of South Carolina, Columbia, SC
Mitchell L. Yell, who received his doctoral degree from the University of Minnesota, is the Fred and Francis Lester Palmetto Chair in Teacher Education and a professor in special education at the University of South Carolina. His professional interests include special education law, individualized education program development, classroom management, and parent involvement in special education. Dr. Yell has published 112 journal articles, 4 textbooks, 26 book chapters and has conducted numerous workshops on various aspects of special education law.

Foreword

"How do I know if what teachers are doing in that classroom is the right thing?"
"I'm not trained in the area of autism."
"I don't know what to look for."

These are often the comments that building principals and local special education administrators make when trying to determine if the services for their students with autism spectrum disorder (ASD) are effective. The Evidence-Based Practice Classroom Observation Tool (EBP COT) offers an excellent tool for these administrators and school leaders to address and assess practices and services that their school offers for students with autism. The tool incorporates evidence-based practices from national resources into a user-friendly and manageable tool. Practitioners will appreciate the one-page resource that assists with creating a vision for quality learning environments for students on the autism spectrum.

With a teacher shortage in all content areas, but in particular, in a field like autism, utilizing professional development resources goes a long way to support stability in teacher retention and increasing student outcomes. Drs. Carnahan and Lowrey have given us a resource that school leaders can use to develop a framework for professional development. The EBP COT also makes way for caregiver participation—a means for the entire team to have active engagement in the individualized education program (IEP) process. School leaders are charged with maximizing time spent on high-quality professional development, while at the same time meeting individual needs, sometimes in large group settings and other times during smaller student team meetings.

Each of the chapters is well-structured and includes clear introductions, objectives, and reflection questions. The explanation of the unique cognitive processes that individuals with autism demonstrate is powerful. The authors take apart each of the cognitive domains and explain the domains in detail through accessible and illustrative case studies. The authors masterfully bring information together for big-picture learning, all the while setting the foundation for why the evidence-based practices are essential for improving student outcomes. This structure is especially critical for adult learners if we are to translate that content into essential learning for students.

I look forward to walking into schools and being able to share this book with principals, administrators, families, and others who want to support teams with creating effective programming for students with ASD. I am confident that this resource will give all educational leaders and stakeholders the best roadmap for successful integration of evidence-based practices and supports for students with autism. Well done Christi and Alisa!

Brooke Carson, Ph.D., State Autism Specialist
Colorado Department of Education

Foreword

Succeeding as an educational leader in the contemporary school environment requires constant diligence to evolving research and policy. The skills honed in the classroom and the experience gathered through years of teaching only provide one component of the complex and dynamic web of expertise administrators must possess. To fully reach their potential as educational leaders, administrators must commit to a career of their own continuing education that requires constant updating and advancement. They recognize that the success of their students, teachers, and staff relies in a large part on their ability to harness everyone's talents and motivate them to work as a team.

For many administrators, understanding special education and succeeding with students with disabilities represents a challenge that is unique from their own experience. A teacher turned administrator may not have had an opportunity to become versed in all aspects of special education. A special education teacher turned administrator often only has worked in a narrow area of disability (e.g., learning disability). In any case, when an administrator steps in to lead, he or she must be prepared to take responsibility for the education of all students and support all teachers.

To fully prepare for the success of all students, administrators must understand the learning needs of their diverse population of students. Students with ASD represent one part of that diversity, and, within the population identified as having ASD, there is great heterogeneity in terms of the level and type of support needed to succeed.

Understanding the intersection of these needs and the federal regulations requires vigilance for the protection of the students' educational rights. When administrators understand a student's needs and what the law provides, they also have to be in a position to support their teachers in identification of evidence-based practices appropriate to those learners' needs. The past two decades have demonstrated tremendous growth in the number of evidence-based practices for enhancing learning, but the list of practices continually evolves as researchers improve on practices and learn more about how individuals with ASD learn. For an administrator, their biggest asset in this area is not knowing every practice but knowing how to separate the wheat from the chaff.

A school district's depth and breadth of knowledge related to learning needs, law, and evidence-based practice cannot rest on the shoulders of a single individual but must be distributed in a manner that allows a district to build suitable capacity to fully educate all students. That capacity building requires a commitment to ongoing collaborative professional development and learning across a district. Drs. Carnahan and Lowrey have compiled an excellent resource for administrators at any stage in their career who want to expand their knowledge and skills related to supporting students with ASD.

Drs. Carnahan and Lowrey's broad range of experiences and expertise, coupled with the highly talented scholars they have invited to join them, have allowed them to produce a valuable guide for administrators looking to strengthen their programming for students with ASD. I am excited about this book because as I work with administrators to support their students with autism, I have always looked for a resource to put in their hands that will function as a durable reference. I believe that Drs. Carnahan and Lowrey have filled that need.

Kevin M. Ayres, Ph.D., BCBA-D
The University of Georgia

Preface

We are excited to put this text in the hands of school leaders, practitioners, and families. The information offered throughout is based on our experiences of what those in K–12 settings need to serve students with autism spectrum disorder (ASD) and other developmental disabilities in inclusive settings. Having worked with teachers, teacher leaders/mentors, principals, and district leaders, we have realized that special education is overwhelming for most; drilling down to those services that are most effective for students with ASD can be even more intimidating. The impetus of this text is to provide a "nuts and bolts" approach to serving students. This is not meant to be an all-inclusive text on the field of ASD or developmental disabilities. Instead, this is meant to provide guidelines that should enhance educational settings for these students.

The guidelines we present are not intended to be used as an evaluation tool but rather as a formative tool on which leaders in education can inform and shape services for students with ASD. We call our tool the EBP COT. EBP stands for evidence-based practices. The goal of the tool is to evaluate if these are being implemented in the classroom. COT refers to the Classroom Observation Tool that we created using the evidence-based practices. Together, this it what informs our work. Chapter 1 provides a detailed user guide for the entire text.

This work has been informed by teachers, paraprofessionals, teacher leaders, principals, district leaders, and ASD specialists. It has been applied in practice and refined to meet the needs of K–12 practitioners and those who advise them. We hope you are able to use it effectively to guide and improve practices in your educational settings serving the needs of students with ASD and other developmental disabilities.

Acknowledgments

We wish to extend our gratitude and thanks to the individuals with ASD and their families from whom we have learned the importance of commitment to quality programming, supports, and collaboration. We would also like to express our thanks to the educators and school leaders who set the foundation for this text by asking questions and looking for practical solutions to collaborative problem solving in support of individuals with ASD. We are thankful to the current/former facilitators of the Louisiana Autism Spectrum and Related Disabilities (LASARD) project for feedback provided early on in this process.

Thank you to the individuals who contributed writing to this book—we are grateful for your collegiality and friendship. We would like to thank the team at Brookes Publishing Company. We are grateful for the opportunity to share our work with a broad audience. We would especially like to thank Rebecca Lazo, now at the Institute for Community Inclusion, and Jolynn Gower, who helped move the text into and through the final stages. We are grateful for your ongoing feedback and support.

Last, we would like to thank our families who support and encourage our work, even when it means they make sacrifices.

Introduction

"I'll know it when I see it, but right now, I don't have a clue what 'it' is." We heard these words spoken by an elementary school principal several years ago. We were together in his office discussing strategies for supporting students with **autism spectrum disorder (ASD)** across several grade levels in his school. The principal knew they needed to improve the educational and social opportunities of learners with ASD, but he felt frustrated. He was not sure where to begin and did not have a lot of time for learning new practices. As we interacted with the principal and others like him, it became clear that although professional development for teachers was critical, principals and other school leaders also needed more information regarding a quality program for students with ASD. These leaders needed more than a list of web resources or a day-long workshop; they needed clear, concise information delivered in a user-friendly format. The idea for this book and the Evidence-Based Practice Classroom Observation Tool (EBP COT) discussed in Chapter 4 was born out of this need.

In developing this text, our goal was to provide leaders in today's schools with a systematic approach for building quality educational experiences for students with ASD. Leaders include district-level administrators, building principals, special education administrators in districts and buildings, curriculum or instructional coaches, and all other individuals who support those teaching students with ASD. Going forward, we will refer to individuals in these groups as leaders. Although intended for school leaders, this text may also serve as a valuable resource for other individuals, including family members, classroom teachers and other professionals, and preservice teachers and professionals.

THE BIG IDEAS IN THIS BOOK

- The belief that all individuals with ASD have the capacity to learn, contribute to their communities, and engage in meaningful social relationships, given the necessary structures and supports, is at the heart of *Facilitating Evidence-Based Practice for Students with ASD*. School leaders play a critical role in ensuring these positive outcomes. Although they are responsible for ensuring quality programs for students with ASD, identifying the appropriate structures and supports can be overwhelming (Livanis, Benvenuto, Mertturk, & Hanthorn, 2013). The purpose of this text is to provide school leaders, educators, and families with an accessible resource for creating engaging learning environments that promote positive behavior and academic growth for individuals with ASD. To this end, we will address the following themes throughout this book: ASD is a neurological, or brain-based, disorder. Students with ASD do not choose to demonstrate differences. The characteristics of ASD drive the behaviors seen academically and socially.

- Federal legislation requires schools to provide quality programming for students with ASD. School leaders positively influence outcomes for these students when they are committed to building quality programs.

- Learners with ASD require specific **evidence-based practices** to be successful in school. School leaders are able to support teachers and other professionals in identifying and implementing appropriate evidence-based practices when they understand the brain–behavior connections in ASD.

- A systematic, collaborative leadership approach is the foundation for implementing evidence-based practices across classrooms and schools. School leaders are the backbone of collaborative environments that promote growth for students and teachers.

Autism, Law, and the Role of School Leaders

The Individuals with Disabilities Education Improvement Act (IDEA) of 2004 (PL108-446) requires that students with ASD receive quality instruction in the **least restrictive environment** (LRE); students with ASD must have access to and make progress in the general education curriculum. Commitment and quality are equally important to the principles of placement and access (McLeskey, Waldron, Spooner, & Algozzine, 2014). Thus, school leaders must commit to meeting the needs of students with ASD, including those with the most significant communication, sensory, and behavioral differences. Commitment alone is not enough, however; understanding the needs of students with ASD and specific practices that support their success is essential. This understanding can then serve as the foundation for collaborating with others to create effective learning environments and quality educational programming for students with ASD.

ASD Is a Brain-Based Disorder

The American Psychological Association (APA; 2013) released revised diagnostic criteria for ASD. Although the specifics of the diagnostic criteria are discussed in Chapter 1, it is worth noting that a medical diagnosis of ASD requires that an individual demonstrate social-communication/interaction differences and restricted or repetitive patterns of behavior, interests, or actions across environments. These diagnostic criteria are important, but understanding that ASD is a neurological or brain-based disorder that substantially influences how students learn and behave in school settings is perhaps more important. Although ASD is defined by differences in social-communication and repetitive behaviors, actions, or thoughts (APA, 2013), many students with ASD also experience other significant differences that influence learning and behavior throughout the school day, including:

- High levels of anxiety
- Difficulty making a transition from one activity to another
- Challenges with planning and organization
- Differences in memory and attention

Students with ASD cannot typically change or control these differences, even though it may be what they want. Thus, education teams designing quality programs must strive to proactively address the needs of students with ASD through environmental design, visual supports, and a variety of other proactive, positive interventions. Students with ASD can be successful when they are actively engaged in well-organized learning environments—a well-structured environment can often be the difference between a student who is actively engaged in learning and one who is anxious, stressed, or completely disengaged.

Evidence-Based Practices: The Foundation for Quality Programming

Creating quality programs that promote academic and social success for students with ASD during and after their school years begins with evidence-based practices. Evidence-based practices are the "practices or programs shown by high quality research to have meaningful effects on student outcomes" (Cook & Odom, 2013, p. 136). The National Professional Development Center (NPDC) on ASD issued a report delineating 27 evidence-based practices (Wong et al., 2014). The necessity of these evidence-based practices, many of which will be discussed in Chapter 3, cannot be overstated—they are critical for creating successful learning environments for students with ASD.

Understanding evidence-based practices is critical for school leaders. Cook and Odom suggested, however, "EBPs are not guaranteed to work for everyone" (2013, p. 137). Awareness of factors such as teacher knowledge and student differences that influence the success of individual evidence-based practices is equally important (McLeskey & Billingsley, 2008; Simpson, McKee, Teeter, & Beytien, 2007). The EBP COT, which is a tool for identifying the foundational practices necessary for all quality programming, will help teams identify interventions that are already in place and prioritize areas for growth and development. For example, an educator and administrator might each complete the EBP COT and compare results. They can use their shared results to set an action plan of specific steps for implementing additional, important practices. We will describe the evidence-based practices included in the EBP COT and approaches for using the tool in a variety of settings (e.g., for planning, for continuous improvement) throughout the text. In addition, we will provide strategies for helping all teachers understand and implement these practices to meet the needs of students with ASD across the spectrum.

Leadership and Collaboration in Quality Programming

Real change, the kind that makes a significant difference in the lives of people, often occurs slowly. It involves both top-down (e.g., policies at state and district levels) and bottom-up activities (e.g., individual classroom and school levels) (Cook & Odom, 2013) and depends on the ability of school leaders to motivate others, build commitment, and create positive conditions for teachers and other professionals (Leithwood, Harris, & Hopkins, 2008). Thus, investing in supporting and developing staff is one of the single greatest things school leaders can do to positively affect change for learners with ASD. The EBP COT is one tool for supporting and developing staff capacity and quality programming.

THE EBP COT

The EBP COT calls on evidence-based practices from the NPDC on ASD, the **Council for Exceptional Children's** (CEC) competencies for teachers of students with ASD, and the National Autism Center (NAC). Both content validity and reliability data support use across grade levels (K–high school) and in inclusive and special education classroom settings (Carnahan, Lowrey, & Snyder, 2014).

The tool includes three broad categories for environmental, instructional, and communication supports. Environmental considerations include organization of the physical environment, visual schedules, and behavioral supports. Instructional considerations address strategies that promote active engagement and individualized instruction. Communication factors address the need for systematic social-communication instruction for all learners with ASD across the school day.

The danger in writing a book such as this and in promoting a tool like the EBP COT is that it could be used as a tool for evaluating teacher effectiveness. The EBP COT is not intended to be a teacher evaluation tool or a comprehensive list for evaluating programs for students with ASD. Rather, it is a tool for assessing classroom environments and supporting teachers and other professionals in effectively implementing evidence-based practices for students across the autism spectrum. The EBP COT was designed to support systematic planning, assessment, and ongoing development of evidence-based practices that are the foundation of quality educational settings.

Suggestions for Educational Leaders

The EBP COT was developed for school leaders, using feedback from school leaders. The intention is to provide a user-friendly list of the practices necessary for quality programming in educational settings. It is a **collaboration** tool designed to help school leaders support new and seasoned educators. The EBP COT could be used in many way—as a planning tool for new education professionals or those new to serving students with ASD, a tool for assessing strengths and growth opportunities in educational settings already serving students with ASD, a tool for guiding professional development, or a combination of all of these.

The EBP COT provides a foundation for new education professionals, or those new to working with students with ASD, for identifying the practices expected in the educational setting and then locating professional development materials or opportunities to support the implementation of these practices. For example, school leaders might share the EBP COT with the new educator or the educator new to working with students with ASD, asking, "What do you already know about these practices? In what areas do you have the most/least amount of knowledge?" The leader could then select areas to target for development. Targeting one section of the EBP COT at a time with the new professional is another option. After ensuring the individual has sufficient knowledge to implement the strategy, the school leader could ask the professional to demonstrate how the EBP COT is being implemented or will be implemented, if the classroom is not yet operating. The school leader might even identify other professionals who excel in implementing specific strategies or practices to develop mentoring relationships for the new professional.

School leaders can use the EBP COT with educators already serving students with ASD as the foundation for collaborating on program development. For example, school leaders might invite teachers, paraeducators, and related services professionals to self-assess their own strengths and growth opportunities with the EBP COT. Other professionals or colleagues, including school leaders, could also observe the educational environment and discuss similarities or differences between the self-assessment and the outsider observation. Professionals can identify what is working well, growth opportunities, and concrete next steps for improving their educational programming.

Last, school leaders could use the EBP COT as a tool for guiding professional development for individual professionals, across classrooms and settings, or even across school districts. For example, school leaders could use the EBP COT to observe classrooms or other settings and identify areas for development for individual teachers, professionals, or paraeducators, or they might identify common strengths and opportunities for growth across settings. Based on these observations, school leaders can then gain access to a variety of resources that aid in professional development, including online professional development, educators or coaches with particular strengths, and study groups or professional learning communities.

Suggestions for Preservice and Practicing Professionals

The EBP COT provides preservice educators with a blueprint for understanding and implementing the supports necessary for creating high-quality programming for students with ASD. Simply being able to identify evidence-based practices while in schools may be a valuable first experience for preservice educators. Based on observations, preservice professionals can ask questions to understand why some interventions are in place or how they are implemented for individual students. Preservice educators might also identify specific practices to implement in one-to-one or small-group settings to gain experience before implementing with larger numbers of students. Similarly, preservice education professionals could identify specific areas in which they already have knowledge and practices with which they have limited experience. Based on this reflection, they can look for additional information, observation opportunities, or resources to deepen knowledge across the domains and specific indicators.

Many of the ways practicing educators and other professionals use the EBP COT parallel school leader use. Educators might use the EBP COT as a planning tool when they structure their classroom environments and systems before beginning the academic school year. Professionals might also use the EBP COT as an ongoing self-assessment and reflection tool throughout the year. Similarly, education professionals might ask others for feedback in certain categories, especially in categories they personally feel offer the greatest opportunities for growth. Or, they might use the EBP COT as a tool for structuring mentoring relationships or conversations. Last, professionals currently serving students with ASD might use the EBP COT as a problem-solving tool when a student is struggling. The tool could serve as a resource for identifying environmental factors needed to support students' engagement and learning.

Suggestions for Families

A common language or way to talk about how to create the optimal setting for a student with ASD can often serve as the foundation for collaborative problem solving. The EBP COT can provide a starting point for families to talk with school personnel about the supports their children need. During times of transition, such as those that occur between grades or schools, it can be difficult to paint a picture of the supports that helped a student be successful. Families can use the EBP COT to begin conversations about how to most effectively support their children before (i.e., identify, communicate, plan for the most important practices on the checklist), during (i.e., provide the kinds of supports necessary during the transition process), and after the transition (i.e., do what is essential to promote long-term engagement, learning, and independence).

In addition to big transitions that often occur alongside a life change, such as a move or graduation from one grade to another, transitions occur throughout the school day. These transitions often mean a change in personnel or setting. Some students with ASD manage these transitions with ease. Other students, however, find it easier to focus and participate in some settings over others. Families can use the EBP COT to facilitate conversations about why these differences occur and identify the kinds of supports necessary for increasing success across all activities in the school day.

The EBP COT can be helpful beyond the school setting as well. School is only one small part of an individual's life—equally important are community and family. Active participation in one's community promotes feelings of connectedness and a sense of belonging. Some community activities are easier than others for individuals with ASD to gain access to, however. Families could use the EBP COT as a tool for talking with other service providers (e.g., summer camps, child care, church programs) about the kinds of strategies needed for an individual to participate in different settings.

WHAT THIS BOOK HAS TO OFFER

Quality educational experiences play a crucial role in outcomes for individuals with ASD after high school. Educational leaders must ensure positive school experiences for these students and provide them with the instruction necessary for academic, social, and life skill success. Creating high-quality programs is one of the best ways to do this. This book will help you understand the cognitive profile of individuals with ASD and the evidence-based practices that support these children's needs.

In Chapter 1, school leaders will learn about the unique characteristics and challenges that students with ASD face, gaining a better understanding of these children's brain-based, neurological differences. Chapter 2 is a discussion of the laws and regulations governing the education of children with ASD—an introduction to key legislation that every school leader needs to know as well as a description of duties and responsibilities in serving students. Chapter 3 answers the fundamental question, "What is an evidence-based practice?" After defining evidence-based practices, this chapter specifically introduces proven practices for students with ASD and provides guidelines on how to recognize evidence-based practices in action. The EBP COT, introduced in Chapter 4, provides the guidelines and foundational knowledge for organizing classrooms and other educational settings to meet the unique needs of students with ASD. Finally, Chapter 5 helps leaders think about and develop strategies for ensuring implementation of evidence-based practices across classrooms, schools, and educational systems.

To enhance functionality and guide you through the book's contents, each chapter begins by telling you what important questions the chapter will answer. The "Questions This Chapter Will Answer" opener previews the most important things you will learn and gives you a glimpse of what new ideas you will discover. Additionally, important terms are highlighted throughout the text, and defined in the glossary. Attending to these terms will help you increase your familiarity with language you might encounter regarding educational policy and programming for students with ASD. Finally, each chapter concludes with a few thought-provoking reflection questions inviting you to apply new concepts and ideas to your work.

Our goal is for this book to serve as a concise, accessible reference guide for school leaders looking to ensure that every student with ASD benefits from thoughtful educational planning and well-chosen supports.

REFERENCES

American Psychological Association. (2013). *Diagnostic and statistical manual of mental disorders* (5th ed.). Washington, DC: Author.

Carnahan, C., Lowrey, K. A., & Snyder, K. (2014). Development of a standardized benchmark assessment tool to facilitate EBP for students with ASD. *DADD Online Journal: Research to Practice, 1*(1), 103–120.

Cook, B., & Odom, S. (2013). Evidence-based practices and implementation science in special education. *Exceptional Children, 79*(2), 135–144.

Elliott, S. N., & Clifford, M. (2014). *Principal assessment: Leadership behaviors known to influence schools and the learning of all students* (Document No. LS-5). Retrieved from http://ceedar.education.ufl.edu/wp-content/uploads/2014/09/LS-5_FINAL_09-26-14.pdf

Leithwood, K., Harris, A., & Hopkins, D. (2008). Seven strong claims about successful school leadership. *School Leadership and Management, 28*(1), 27–42.

Livanis, A., Benvenuto, S., Mertturk, A., & Hanthorn, C. (2013). Treatment integrity in autism spectrum disorder interventions. In S. Goldstein & J. Naglieri (Eds.), *Interventions for autism spectrum disorders: Translating science into practice* (pp. 19–38). New York, NY: Springer.

McLeskey, J., & Billingsley, B. S. (2008). How does the quality and stability of the teaching force influence the research-to-practice gap? A perspective on the teacher shortage in special education. *Remedial and Special Education, 29*(5), 293–305.

McLeskey, J., Waldron, N. L., Spooner, F., & Algozzine, B. (2014). *Handbook of effective inclusive schools: Research and practice*. New York, NY: Routledge.

Simpson, R. L., McKee, M., Teeter, D., & Beytien, A. (2007). Evidence-based methods for children and youth with autism spectrum disorders: Stakeholder issues and perspectives. *Exceptionality, 15*(4), 203–217.

Wong, C., Odom, S., Hume, K., Cox, A., Fettig, A., Kucharczyk, S., . . . Schultz, T. (2014). *Evidence-based practices for children, youth, and young adults with autism spectrum disorder*. Chapel Hill, NC: University of North Carolina, Frank Porter Graham Child Development Institute, Autism Evidence-Based Practice Review Group.

*To the children, families, and professionals with
whom we work, and from whom we continue to learn*

*To our families, whose ongoing support
is critical to our work*

1 Understanding the Learning and Behavioral Needs of Students With ASD

Christina R. Carnahan, Kate Doyle, and K. Alisa Lowrey

QUESTIONS THIS CHAPTER WILL ANSWER

1. How does autism spectrum disorder (ASD) affect thinking and behavior?
2. What are some challenges students with ASD face in school?
3. What are some basic supports and intervention strategies that can help students with ASD in the classroom?

ASD is characterized by differences in **social-communication** and repetitive behaviors or interests. Although these differences can pose challenges, individuals with ASD can be highly successful at home, at school, and in their communities when they are given the right supports (Mesibov, Shea, & Schopler, 2005). This chapter describes the cognitive profile common in ASD and how these characteristics influence engagement and learning at school. Understanding this profile will allow a school leader, classroom teacher, parent, or other support person to communicate about why the interventions described in this book are so important, which is critical for getting all team members invested in implementing **best practices** for students with ASD in classrooms, in schools, and across districts.

WHAT IS ASD?

Both diagnostic criteria and individual cognitive theories help explain the differences common in ASD (Williams et al., 2012). Together, the diagnostic and cognitive profile can result in the academic and social challenges sometimes seen in schools (Mesibov et al.,

2005). A lot of ways an individual engages at school is a direct reflection of how ASD manifests in his or her life. If an individual with ASD acts in ways that seem disruptive or challenging, it can be helpful to remember the actions are often a direct manifestation of differences in how he or she perceives the environment.

ASD is a spectrum disorder resulting in a wide range of strengths and needs (Heflin & Simpson, 1998). Specific diagnostic criteria include social-communication challenges and circumscribed or narrow interests or behavior (American Psychiatric Association [APA], 2013). The social-communication differences may manifest in schools as difficulty with relationships and verbal and nonverbal communication challenges such as appropriately using or interpreting vocabulary, gestures, or facial expressions. The terms *repetitive behavior* or *restricted interests* refer to a broad category of differences that can include verbal, physical, or cognitive behavior. For example, an individual with ASD may demonstrate repetitive body movement, engage in repeated conversation, or have thoughts dominated by a specific topic while in school.

The next section addresses the specific cognitive theories that inform how ASD is understood. First, it is important to remember that the strengths and needs of individuals with ASD change over the lifetime, just like all people (Mundy, Mastergeorge, & McIntyre, 2012). The characteristics or profile a child with ASD demonstrates today does not dictate how he or she will behave in the future. From this perspective, creating well-structured learning environments, systematically teaching and practicing social-communication skills, and ensuring access to meaningful, appropriately challenging academic tasks are the foundation for both social and academic success.

COGNITIVE THEORIES IN ASD

Three different theories are often used to describe the cognitive differences common in ASD—**executive function (EF), theory of mind (ToM),** and weak **central coherence** (WCC). No single perspective sufficiently explains the cognitive differences in ASD, but the theories collectively clarify some of the cognitive processing often seen in individual with ASD. In addition, these theories can be helpful when planning supportive, effective learning environments for students with ASD. The following sections describe the theories and provide basic strategies and supports that can be used for individuals with ASD. The list below introduces some of the important ideas regarding cognitive processing that will be discussed in the chapter.

- Understanding cognitive differences is the foundation for creating a supportive learning environment for students with ASD.

- Building positive social relationships and creating meaningful, appropriately challenging academic tasks are often the key steps related to promoting positive behavior and learning.

- ASD results in a wide range of strengths and needs across individuals.

- Three different cognitive theories have emerged to explain the behavioral differences ASD presents in individuals:
    - Executive function
    - Theory of mind
    - Weak central coherence

- The social transaction theory of autism also provides helpful insights into the social lives of individuals with ASD at school.

Executive Function

Austin is an eighth-grade student with ASD. He loves music, especially music that comes from nature, such as the sounds whales make. Austin also enjoys helping others, spending time with his family, and going on vacation. He seems to enjoy his academic classes, especially science and, specifically, the marine ecosystem. Austin attends general education classes in which he receives accommodations such as extra time on tests, assistance organizing his notes, and shortened homework assignments. He often struggles, however, to complete assignments, stay organized, and interact with his peers during small-group activities. Austin also participates in a social skills group each week that is led by a speech-language pathologist (SLP) and the school counselor.

Austin walks about a mile home at the end of the school day. Some days it takes him more than 45 minutes to make the walk because he stops to look at pictures of whales on his smart phone or locate online videos of whales. Austin often ends up in tears when he arrives home because he has forgotten an important paper, cannot locate a textbook, or is generally overwhelmed.

Austin is like many adolescents with ASD. He understands the content of his academic classes, but he often struggles because of differences related to EF, which is the ability for people to direct their own attention to solve problems or engage in the day-to-day activities of their lives (Zelazo, Blair, & Willoughby, 2016). Executive function skills allow individuals to "mentally maintain a specified goal" even when distractions are present (Fisher & Happe, 2005, p. 757). EF is an essential aspect of regulating behavior and involves inhibiting responses, emotional control, task initiation, flexible thinking, and persistence (Bass, 2014). The EF challenges Austin faces influence his ability to organize all his materials throughout and at the end of the school day. He quickly becomes overwhelmed when he tries to gather everything he needs for homework, and his disorganization increases as he becomes overwhelmed. So, when he finally arrives home and opens his bag, the materials appear to be shoved in, with one item piled on top of the next.

EF also influences how individuals process and respond to social information. People have to direct their attention to what an individual is saying and doing, while also carefully attending to the environment, in order to understand the social cues of others. In addition, social sophistication requires understanding the rules of each setting, adjusting behavior accordingly, and quickly interpreting and responding to communication breakdowns. The challenges Austin faces in his classes are usually not related to academic activities. Rather, the social demands that vary from class to class are problematic. For example, Austin's science class, which is generally his favorite, involves a lot of small-group and partner work. Austin becomes upset when his classmates do not follow the exact directions or stop listening when he begins talking about the music of whales. Thus, Austin is often anxious before science class, which, in turn, increases his difficulty paying attention, organizing his materials, and working with others. Although Austin is generally a flexible thinker, his ability to think flexibly during partner work significantly decreases. For example, in a recent small-group lab project, two group members were working on different parts of the experiment at the same time. Austin became increasingly upset, repeatedly telling his classmates, "We have to do one first. We have to do one first," even when the teacher tried to reassure him the team could complete both steps at the same time. He became so upset that he struggled to regulate his emotions and nearly lost composure in front of his classmates.

Austin is typically able to function during the school day with minimal support. His EF regulation skills are diminished, however, under stress. Like most students with ASD, Austin would benefit from a variety of EF related interventions (Hill, 2004). **Visual** supports, including schedules, work systems, and video models, are often good options; they can be created flexibly, are portable, and can become more sophisticated as the student grows. Other important interventions include establishing well-organized, predictable environments, teaching flexibility, and helping the students learn strategies for recognizing and managing anxiety.

Linking Anxiety and Executive Function Anxiety is often a major co-occurring challenge for children and young people with ASD (Hollocks et al., 2014). In the example, Austin was hyperfocused on following the directions in a science lab, although it was just fine for the students to complete two steps at once. Theories of anxiety are tied to EF theory; competition between goal-directed attention and perceived negative stimuli or information in the environment exists when an individual is anxious. If a student has an elevated level of anxiety, then there may be a hyperattentiveness to the negative information. Emotions and stress can negatively influence a student's ability to regulate his or her attention and behavior (Zelazo et al., 2016). Thus, supporting students to be flexible and calm needs to be a daily consideration for the education team when serving students with ASD who experience anxiety.

Theory of Mind

Tori is a second-grade student with ASD who has a strong interest in animals, especially giraffes. She reads every book and watches every video her parents and teachers can find. Tori often finds ways to bring the conversation back to giraffes when she talks with peers and school staff, and she will sometimes continue the conversation when a peer walks away.

Ms. Jones, Tori's language arts teacher, explains to the students that they will be working in small groups to create a diorama about a book they read as a class that was about going to summer camp. Ms. Jones talks with the students about how she expects them to work collaboratively to create the diorama, providing explicit directions. After giving the directions, Ms. Jones directs the students to break into small groups and begin working.

Ms. Jones begins circling the classroom once the children begin working. She notices that Tori is sitting with her back to the group, using the materials to create an elaborate giraffe structure. Ms. Jones casually sits down with the group and begins listening to the conversation. When Ms. Jones asks Tori to join the group, Tori explains that she is excited about a new giraffe video her mom borrowed from the library and wants to build a giraffe to go with the video. Tori's peers then chime in, expressing frustration that Tori was hogging the materials and not responding to their invitations to participate. Ms. Jones quickly returns the conversation to Tori, asking her, "Tori, why are your classmates upset?" Tori's response is a look of confusion. She explains, "I'm not sure why they are upset. Look at how cute my giraffe is. I made his tongue almost the exact shade of the new baby giraffe at the zoo." Tori is so focused on her giraffe and own excitement that she has difficulty understanding that her peers and teacher are frustrated, even though they are all sitting with crossed arms and frowns.

Tori clearly did not attend to the body language of the group—crossed arms and a frown—to interpret the perspective of her peers and teacher. This difficulty is referred to as **theory of mind (ToM)**, which is the ability to recognize the thoughts, beliefs, and intentions of others and understand that these differ from person to person. Baron-Cohen, Leslie, and Frith (1985) first introduced the concept of ToM in relation to ASD. It seems that the EF characteristics described in the previous section are closely related to the

ToM characteristics students exhibit (Zelazo et al., 2016). It is likely that the attention, flexibility, and inhibitory differences related to EF then influence the ability of an individual with ASD to incorporate the perspective of others into his or her own behavior.

Ultimately, an individual is able to predict and respond to the behavior of others when he or she attends to the perspectives of others (Baron-Cohen et al., 1985). Tori struggled with the diorama activity because of her intense passion for giraffes. She fully engaged in her own activity rather than shifting her attention from the giraffe to her peers and the task.

When an individual has difficulty moving away from his or her or own perspective or interest, as Tori did, it is likely because of the differences in ToM. The challenges often result in difficulty with the following:

- The pragmatic aspects of language, such as communicative intentions and reading or understanding social situations (Frith, 2008)
- Recognizing, understanding, and empathizing with the perspectives of others (Jones et al., 2005, 2018; Frith, 2008)
- Attending to others because of a strong passion for their own interests
- Identifying their own feelings and thoughts and differentiating these from others (Frith, 2008)

Students with ASD often need consistent and explicit social-communication instruction and well-organized learning environments to be successful in school because of these differences in ToM. For example, Tori's teacher might use social narratives (Whalon, Conroy, Martinez, & Werch, 2015)—individualized stories that describe social situations and how to respond appropriately. Social narratives are an evidence-based practice that can direct the attention of individuals with ASD to the big picture of a situation and the perspectives of others (Wong et al., 2015). Students may be able to engage more fully with the people in their environments when they understand the perspectives of others. In addition, a visual support, such as a written checklist, might help Tori focus on the expected behavior or activities and complete tasks independently. Finally, Tori may also benefit from direct instruction on how to participate in groups. At first, this instruction might focus on the specific steps for participating, but Tori would eventually benefit from strategies she can use during activities to think about others' perspectives and self-monitor her own behavior. Chapter 3 contains links to strategies that support social skills and social competence.

Weak Central Coherence

Ted is a junior in a large public high school and has a passion for airplanes. He spends most of his free time building model airplanes or reading nonfiction manuals on aircrafts. Ted was recently given a writing assignment to read a historical, biographical passage about Orville Wright and discuss the personal and professional adversities that Orville faced while inventing the airplane. Ted wrote a three-page essay on the technical details of three axis control, which would have qualified for a technical manual in the early 1900s. Mr. Sand, Ted's English teacher, is unfamiliar with the technical terms used in the assignment and shares it with Mrs. Rivers, the physics teacher.

Mrs. Rivers explains that Ted accurately and succinctly detailed the Wright brothers' invention, which allowed pilots to maintain flight equilibrium. Ted did not accurately complete the assignment, however, which was to discuss the personal or professional adversities that

Orville Wright faced. Ted is clearly passionate about airplanes, and his teacher attempted to channel the passion into a writing assignment for English class. Unfortunately, reading about the technical details of the aircraft distracted Ted, and he lost sight of the larger assignment to write about the life of Orville Wright.

WCC, the third cognitive theory, may explain Ted's difficulties. Central coherence refers to the ability to focus on the important information in a situation and then use the information appropriately (Quill, 2017). The exact role that WCC plays in cognition for individuals with ASD continues to be debated, but WCC is likely closely related to EF. Students with ASD often struggle to understand the big picture or meaning of an event and may overattend to specific details of an event or topic. They may also be distracted by details or events in an environment (e.g., noise in the background, a flickering light). WCC may manifest in the following ways in a school environment:

- Specialized, often detail-focused, interests
- Strong rote memory or attention to details
- Difficulty generalizing experiences across environments

Students with ASD often have difficulty comprehending and retrieving information in an integrated, meaningful way because of these differences. For example, rather than interpreting information about how the first planes were developed, including the lives of the Wright brothers, Ted was overly focused on specific details about the aircraft. Although Ted had received a good deal of instruction about the big picture, the challenges Orville and Wilbur faced in the early 1900s were completely outside of Ted's attention.

Ted also has difficulty comprehending and integrating information when new information challenges his existing knowledge. For example, when Ted is presented with information that is different from his existing knowledge about airplanes, he often dismisses the information or becomes argumentative, suggesting the new information is incorrect. Although Ted had previous experiences with the writing structures his English teacher expected him to use, he was not able to generalize or apply his knowledge when reading about airplanes.

Ted needs instruction designed to point his attention to the big ideas of what he is learning because of his detail-oriented focus. For example, he may have benefited from a variety of external supports, such as a **task analysis** (Sam & AFIRM, 2015), a **graphic organizer** (Finnegan & Mazin, 2016), and a self-management intervention (Koegel, Park, & Koegel, 2014). Task analysis is a process in which an activity is broken down into small steps to teach the skill (Wong et al., 2015) and can be provided to a student via printed word or auditorily. Self-management is instruction that focuses on accurately recording and monitoring one's own behavior and can be utilized in the form of a self-checklist to complete after writing (Wong et al., 2015).

In addition, Ted needs reminders during instruction about what he is learning and how the new information connects to his existing knowledge. His teacher can use a graphic organizer, which is a visual display that demonstrates relationships among facts, concepts, and ideas, to assist in making these connections (Carnahan & Williamson, 2016). Last, strategies such as **priming,** in which the teacher previews the big idea of a new concept (Smith, 2008) and pairs it with graphic organizers, are also critical to help students with ASD see the big picture.

The concepts of EF, ToM, and WCC help individuals understand the cognitive profile common in ASD. Perhaps more important, these perspectives provide critical insight into how ASD manifests in the lives of children, adolescents, and young adults in school settings. In addition to EF, ToM, and WCC, the transactional social attention model of autism (Mundy et al., 2012) adds another dimension to understanding the challenges students with ASD face in school.

TRANSACTIONAL SOCIAL ATTENTION MODEL OF AUTISM

The ability to prioritize and coordinate attention with other people is a major milestone for all young children. This type of **joint attention** allows young children to assume a common frame of reference with others that makes it possible for social engagement, symbolic and language development, and learning about other people (Mundy et al., 2012). Individuals with ASD have significant differences in how joint attention develops, which affects their ability to share information with others as well as take advantage of social learning opportunities (Mundy et al., 2012).

Lily is a third-grade student with ASD who is fully included in her general education classroom. She is generally successful throughout the day because of the academic interventions her team creates for her. Lily's parents, however, report that she is sad about coming to school and often needs extensive prodding to get out of bed in the morning and often cries all the way to school. When her teacher asks Lily why she does not want to come to school, Lily reports that she does not have any friends and other students are mean to her. Her parents state that Lily often uses scripted language (e.g., unusual word choices from her favorite movies and television shows, uncommon prosody) during times of high stress, and they ask the teacher to pay attention when Lily might be using this type of language at school. Mrs. Brown, Lily's intervention specialist, decides to observe Lily during unstructured times of her day to see if she can make any changes to assist Lily.

Mrs. Brown notes that Lily spends recess circling the perimeter of the playground, and the aides on the playground report to Mrs. Brown that Lily is often "in her own world." She continuously repeats scripts from her favorite movies to herself while flapping her hands. Freeze tag is a very popular game at recess in the third grade. Lily often thinks she is playing and will run around the field; however, no peers ever engage with her. Lily does not try to initiate with classmates to let them know she wants to be part of the game.

After recess, Mrs. Brown observes at lunch, noting that Lily is sitting alone at the end of the table and does not interact with any peers. Although it does not appear that anyone is outright teasing Lily, Mrs. Brown realizes that Lily has few meaningful relationships with peers.

Young children engage in shared interactions with families and peers during early development that provide the foundation for later language and social development. Many young children with ASD, however, often do not engage in these experiences in the same way as their peers. Thus, it is not surprising that Lily has significant social challenges during the school years. Many learners with ASD have difficulty responding in expected ways during academic and nonacademic times because of social competence differences (Bass, 2014). Specifically, these differences may cause challenges in the following areas:

- Difficulty understanding and sharing information with others during social interactions that occur inside and outside the classroom

- Difficulty following, initiating, and joining quick changes in shared attention that comprise social interactions both in and outside the classroom; therefore, students with ASD may avoid or appear awkward in social interactions
- Difficulty attending to topics or social interactions not directly related to topics of interest (Mundy et al., 2012)

These social challenges are likely frustrating for a learner with ASD, and, at times, there may be an outward display of this frustration. Thus, although the primary focus in schools is often the academic or behavioral challenges students with ASD face, addressing social attention differences may support learning in both areas (Ricketts, Jones, Happe, & Charman, 2013). Effective interventions must teach social competence and the ability to acquire, understand, and use social knowledge to respond appropriately to social information.

Individuals with ASD often face many challenges with social competence. Even when students with ASD are immersed in a rich social environment, such as recess, they will often remain isolated without direct intervention due to their inability to take advantage of social learning opportunities. For example, Lily wants to be a part of her peer group but lacks the skills to initiate and maintain peer relationships. Lily's anxiety increases during unstructured times, such as lunch and recess, most likely due to lack of a clear structure or routine. Lily's use of scripted language and repetitive movements increase when she is anxious.

Providing clear guidelines and direct instruction would likely decrease Lily's anxiety over time. For example, a **visual schedule** at recess would help her understand social and behavioral expectations, which would lead to higher levels of engagement. Lily may also benefit from an intervention such as **video modeling,** a video of the targeted behavior to assist in learning a desired skill (Wong et al., 2015). Lily would learn specific playground behaviors or routines through a video model. She could then practice these in a small group before going to recess with her entire class. Combining these social supports with those discussed in the sections on EF and ToM can be critical in helping a student with ASD navigate the social environment and meaningfully participate in school activities.

ASD AND SCHOOL CHALLENGES

School can be challenging for students with ASD due to a complex interplay of social, cognitive, communicative, and learning differences. Heightened anxiety and stress, a struggle to generalize and apply learned skills, problems communicating thoughts and feelings, and explosive behavior all contribute to school difficulties. The following sections demonstrate how anxiety, academics, communication, and explosive behavior are linked in the classroom and summarize the impact of these challenges on students' ability to learn and thrive in school.

Anxiety and Stress

Individuals with ASD often experience high levels of anxiety or stress because of their social and cognitive differences. At least 50% of individuals with ASD have co-occurring anxiety disorder (Storch et al., 2013), and many students with ASD are highly anxious from the minute they enter the building each day (Dunn-Buron, 2014). A variety of activities may be confusing, stressful, or overwhelming for learners with ASD during a typical school day (Mesibov et al., 2005). For example, activities perceived as typical or uncomplicated, such as making transitions, responding to directions, or completing tasks such as homework, can produce high levels of anxiety. Moreover, anxiety appears to magnify the symptoms of ASD, including increased repetitive behavior, sensory difficulties, and impaired social responsiveness (Storch et al., 2013).

Academic Achievement

The way a student with ASD presents behaviorally and socially in school often does not reflect their actual cognitive ability (Mundy et al., 2012). Students with ASD often have different ways of completing tasks and engaging in the classroom (e.g., using black and white thinking, literal interpretations of what is said by peers and school staff, rigidity to routines, difficulty seeing the big picture) (Randi, Newman, & Grigorenko, 2010). It may feel frustrating to the learner and the school that a student may be able to demonstrate a skill, such as **self-regulation** or engagement, in a one-to-one or clinical setting, yet the student is not able to generalize this skill to the classroom environment. It is easier to understand these discrepancies, however, when thinking about the students using the cognitive and social theories previously discussed. Students with ASD often struggle with generalization and may learn a skill in one context; yet, they have trouble transferring and using the skill across several settings. Also, students with ASD often have difficulty filtering what information (both social and academic) is relevant and useful in a school setting.

Communicating Thoughts and Feelings

Many learners with ASD will have difficulty communicating their feelings and thoughts verbally or through **augmentative and alternative communication (AAC) systems**—methods used to supplement or replace speech or writing for those with language impairments. These systems can look like speech-generating devices (SGDs) or visual communication boards. School staff must use their observations to help decipher what the student's behavior is communicating. Many traditional behavior plans for students with ASD will often neglect the skills they need to learn to manage their anxiety, and the plans may not address underdeveloped social and communication skills (Minahan & Rappaport, 2012).

School staff need to recognize that social-communicative behavior requires social understanding. Skills need to be supported and built in an appropriate developmental sequence. Many students with ASD will have anxiety before, during, and after social situations. For example, a student who does not know how to appropriately initiate with a peer may struggle extensively with many general education classroom expectations, such as collaborating and negotiating with peers or engaging in group discussions. Free play, recess, and unstructured time are often the most challenging times for students with ASD. School staff can support students by increasing structure (e.g., visual schedules, social scripts) and staff and peer support during these times. Building social competence through direct social-communication instruction will build success and decrease anxiety.

Explosive Behavior

The complicated interplay of cognitive and social challenges or differences in ASD can, at times, result in explosive behavior in students with ASD, including both physically and verbally aggressive behaviors. Students with ASD must understand the learning situation; apply the expectations of the learning situation to their own thoughts, feelings, and behaviors; and demonstrate an understanding of the thoughts, feelings, and behaviors of others to be successful in school. Challenges with perspective taking, working memory, response inhibition, seeing the big picture, and emotional control can often cause a situation to quickly escalate into explosive behavior. Learners with ASD are consistently asked to demonstrate abilities that are not fully developed, underdeveloped, or simply different throughout the school day, and they are expected to collaboratively engage and learn in a social group setting every day despite their social-communication challenges. Explosive behavior is a message and rarely a conscious choice. The message is that a student does not understand the environment or can no longer manage his or her anxiety. It is critical that educators remember these challenges when addressing the explosive or challenging behaviors of students with ASD.

BRINGING IT ALL TOGETHER: ASD AND IMPLICATIONS FOR EDUCATIONAL PROGRAMMING

The cognitive and social differences that students with ASD present have many academic implications. The following recommendations can support education teams in creating valuable learning situations for learners with ASD:

1. *Focus on engagement.* Teachers should make instructional decisions based on the student's unique needs and individual social and cognitive profile. It is integral for educators to build on a student's success and strive for continuous student engagement. Researchers and policy makers have identified active engagement as a crucial element in effective programming for students with ASD (Iovannone, Dunlap, Huber, & Kincaid, 2003; National Research Council, 2001; Ruble & Robson, 2007).

2. *Develop structures and routines that make the student with ASD feel calm and safe, and the student will be more available for learning new academic content* (Stoppelbein, Biasini, Pennick, & Greening, 2016).

3. *Implement systematic instruction.* Systematic instruction involves specific or direct instruction of specific skills in a trial-based format (Collins, 2012). Instruction should also include evidence-based practices such as task analysis and visual supports. A task analysis, which breaks down a task into small discrete steps (Alberto & Troutman, 2009), and visual supports, which includes a written visual schedule of the academic task, pictures, labels, or organization systems (Hume, 2013), are key to supporting learners with ASD. Teachers should become skilled at explicitly leading students to the big picture by reminding students what they are learning and connecting their new knowledge to the big picture (Carnahan & Williamson, 2016).

4. *Use topics of interest to support instruction and increase academic learning.* Using a student's special interest can increase instructional effectiveness (Boyd, Conroy, Mancil, Nakao, & Alter, 2007; Mancil & Pearl, 2008; Porter, 2012), particularly for students who have rigid interests or difficulty maintaining attention.

5. *Balance social and academic demands.* As previously noted, many learners with ASD experience school at a heightened state of arousal due to anxiety, which may limit the student's ability to be available for learning and interacting (Prizant, Wetherby, Rubin, & Laurent, 2003). A student with high anxiety is at risk of falling behind academically because he or she is distracted and has impaired working memory skills when anxious (Hopko, Crittendon, Grant, & Wilson, 2005). If the social demand for many learners with ASD goes up (e.g., unexpected change in classroom routine, collaborative learning game, group discussion), then the cognitive demand must go down. Many teachers may use games to reinforce previous learning. Many students with ASD, however,

often do not easily understand the rules of games (Solish, Perry, & Minnes, 2010), and it may be difficult for learners with ASD to grasp any new content while also attempting to participate in an activity that requires social engagement. Developing a concrete plan regarding how students with ASD participate in the game is critical. Conversely, if cognitive demands are high in a particular academic task, then students with ASD may have difficulty with other components of the assignment, such as writing, maintaining engagement, or verbally answering questions. It is critical to demonstrate flexibility, prioritize skills, and carefully plan instruction to promote academic success when teaching students with ASD.

6. *Teach missing skills to support positive behavior.* Many behavior support plans often focus on the reinforcement of appropriate behavior. Systematically teaching students how to demonstrate these desired behaviors when they are flooded with anxiety is critical (Minahan & Rappaport, 2012). Students with ASD need direct, explicit social skill instruction. Social skill instruction should be individualized, systematic, and targeted in a variety of settings to promote generalization. The importance of teaching social skills cannot be overemphasized. A lack of social skills for a student with ASD that leads to unexpected social behavior can often be judged severely by peers, caregivers, and school staff (Dunn-Buron, 2014).

7. *Teach self-regulation, or the ability to manage behaviors, thoughts, and emotions and effectively control one's reactions.* Consider positively reinforcing social and self-regulation throughout the school day (Minahan & Rappaport, 2012). School staff may have to change their mind-set when it comes to aggressive or disruptive behavior (Dunn-Buron, 2014); punitive measures such as suspension or removal to the office are often ineffective and may reinforce the behavior the student is exhibiting, particularly if the behavior serves as an escape function. Proactive strategies teach replacement behaviors and promote decreased levels of anxiety, which may minimize behavioral challenges and increase engagement and learning.

Although an expansion in knowledge regarding effective instructional practices for students with ASD has occurred since the mid-2000s, no one strategy or set of approaches supports all individuals with ASD. Rather, students with ASD benefit from a range of practices that account for their individual cognitive and social strengths and needs (Prizant et al., 2003). Many students with ASD are capable of learning in natural and inclusive environments when appropriate accommodations and modifications support their distinctive social and learning characteristics (Prizant et al., 2003). Students with ASD will continue to change and grow over time. Thus, designing learning environments that account for their unique and evolving needs is critical for preparing them for the next stage in their life, no matter what it may be.

ADDITIONAL RESOURCES

Web Sites

- Autism Speaks
  https://www.autismspeaks.org

- Center for Disease Control, Autism Spectrum Disorder
  https://www.cdc.gov/ncbddd/autism/index.html

- National Autism Center
  http://www.nationalautismcenter.org

- SCERTS
  http://www.scerts.com

Recommended Reading

Attwood, T. (2008). An overview of autism spectrum disorders. In K. D. Buron & P. Wolfberg (Eds.), *Learners on the autism spectrum: Preparing highly qualified educators* (pp. 18–43). Shawnee Mission, KS: Autism Asperger.

Carnahan, C., & Williamson, P. (2010). Autism, cognition, and reading. In C. Carnahan & P. Williamson (Eds.), *Quality literacy instruction for students with autism spectrum disorders* (pp. 21–44). Shawnee Mission, KS: Autism Asperger.

Mundy, P., & Mastergeorge, A. (Eds.). (2012). *Educational interventions for students with autism.* New York, NY: Wiley.

Prizant, B. M., Wetherby, A. M., Rubin, E., Laurent, A. C., & Rydell, P. J. (2006). *The SCERTS® model: A comprehensive educational approach for children with autism spectrum disorders.* Baltimore, MD: Paul H. Brookes Publishing Co.

Zelazo, P. D., Blair, C. B., & Willoughby, M. T. (2016). Executive function: Implications for education. NCER 2017-2000. *National Center for Education Research.* Available from https://ies.ed.gov/ncer/pubs/20172000/pdf/20172000.pdf

REFLECTION QUESTIONS

1. Think of a learner you know with ASD. In what ways might ToM, EF, and WCC affect the learner? List five concrete examples of how these cognitive differences might manifest in a classroom setting.

2. Think of a learner you know with ASD. What are some of this student's biggest classroom challenges? What are his or her needs? Consider some of the general supports and strategies discussed in this chapter and begin brainstorming some intervention strategies that might be helpful for this individual.

3. What is your school's approach to handling explosive behavior in the classroom? Do educators have effective behavior plans in place? What work still needs to be done in your school around ASD and explosive behavior?

4. Discuss the challenges of meeting the needs of learners with ASD of various ages and ability levels in your school. Brainstorm ways administrators and teachers can better meet these challenges in your school.

5. What interventions in this chapter could easily be implemented in a general education setting? Are there any that you think could not? Why?

6. What role does anxiety play in ASD? What supports are available for ASD learners with high anxiety in your school? Who could/does provide these supports? What supports may need to be added?

2 Laws Every Leader Needs to Know

A Look at Legislation, Regulations, Case Law, and Individuals With ASD

K. Alisa Lowrey, Mitchell L. Yell, and Gregory W. Smith

QUESTIONS THIS CHAPTER WILL ANSWER

1. What laws govern educational services for students with ASD?
2. What services must schools provide to students with ASD?
3. How does case law affect services for students with ASD?

As a leader, understanding both the letter and spirit of the law is critical to ensuring success in school and to fully grasp the depth and breadth of services that should be provided to students. Three types of law exert a profound influence on the educational system—**legislation, regulations,** and **case law.** Legislation in education, which can either be at the state or federal level, typically mandates the provision of services or access to services that previously did not exist. After legislation becomes a law, that law may be reauthorized or updated to further define the scope of services or access to services. A state law must align with a federal law when they both exist in a particular area. A state law may actually provide more rights than a federal law, but it cannot provide or do less. Educational leaders should be familiar with state and federal legislation because both influence their work.

In addition, the educational leader must also be well versed in the specific regulations that are written into legislative law. Regulations are detailed procedures and protocol for how a law should be implemented. A law tends to be general in nature when it is passed by Congress. Congress then delegates power to the appropriate administrative agencies, such as the U.S. Department of Education, to create specific regulations describing how to implement the law. A similar process occurs at the state level. These regulations supply specifics to the general content of the law and provide procedures by which the law can be enforced. Regulations have the force of law and must be followed.

Case law is the third type of law affecting educational practice. *Case law* refers to the published opinions of judges that arise from court cases in which the judges interpret legislation and regulations and then apply the law to the specific facts of a case. A body of case law begins to form when numerous decisions occur in a specific area (e.g., **least restrictive environments [LREs]** for students with disabilities). This case law helps to clarify and define the legislation and regulations. The court systems exist at both a state and federal level, and the structure of courts at the state and federal level are similar. Most cases regarding IDEA are heard in the federal courts; therefore, rulings at the federal level exert the greatest influence on special education. Three levels of courts operate in the federal system—U.S. district courts, U.S. courts of appeals for the various circuits, and the U.S. Supreme Court.

Familiarity with educational laws, regulations, and case law ensures that your educational programs and procedures are carried out in a legally sound manner. The purpose of this chapter is to review the provisions of current federal legislation, regulations, and recent case law as they directly affect services for individuals with ASD. This chapter is not meant to be a comprehensive review of each law, regulation, or case. Rather, it is meant to provide an overview of basic guidelines and considerations for daily practice. Resources will be provided for digging deeper when conflicts or questions exist.

THE INDIVIDUALS WITH DISABILITIES EDUCATION ACT

IDEA is the primary federal law defining the supports and services available for individuals with disabilities from birth through age 21. This legislation was initially passed as the Education for All Handicapped Children Act of 1975 (PL 94-142). Revisions have been made in 1986, 1990, 1997, and 2004 (Conroy, Yell, Katsiyannis, & Collins, 2010). IDEA provides the foundation and direction for special education services provided to students with disabilities in publicly funded school systems. The provisions of IDEA also apply to those students with ASD. Several important components of IDEA should be considered when educating students with ASD: **zero reject**, **eligibility, free appropriate public education (FAPE)**, LRE, and **procedural safeguards**. These aspects of the law will affect educational programming for your students with disabilities.

Zero Reject

According to the zero reject principle of IDEA, all students with disabilities eligible for services under IDEA are entitled to special education services regardless of the severity of their disability. All students ages birth through 21 with disabilities or suspected of having disabilities residing in a school district's jurisdiction should be identified, located, and evaluated for special education services. School districts have an affirmative duty to identify, locate, and evaluate these students under **Child Find**, a mandate of IDEA that helps ensure all students in need of services receive the supports they need. Child Find states that an evaluation for special education services is always required when school district personnel become aware of or suspect that a student may need special education. Schoolwide referral processes, in which teachers, counselors, administrators, or any school-based personnel refer a student for possible special education services, are the most typical way to implement Child Find activities. Parents may also refer their child.

Eligibility

Determining eligibility for special education services is another key component of IDEA. A student must be determined eligible under one or more of the 13 categories covered by IDEA, one of which is ASD, for him or her to receive special education services. Special education services include but are not limited to educational services, **related services**, transportation, accommodations, and behavior and social supports. IDEA clearly outlines the eligibility process for all students suspected of having a disability.

- A student must be referred to the school building level support team for an evaluation. Either school personnel or a parent might make the referral, or the student may have been located and identified through one of the school district's Child Find processes.

- The school must secure written consent from the parents/guardians to evaluate the student before any individualized testing outside of general classroom testing is completed. This parental consent must be obtained within 10 days of receiving the initial written request for a referral, or a meeting should take place with parents to discuss their rights and next steps.

- Once consent is secured, the child must be evaluated using several multidisciplinary assessments delivered in his or her native language that demonstrate appropriate psychometric sensitivity to the student's race, gender, and socioeconomic status. One measure cannot be used to determine eligibility. Moreover, evaluations should include a wide variety of tools designed to measure vision and hearing, cognitive levels, adaptive behavior functioning, functional behavior, speech and language, motor functioning, psychological functioning, and social functioning. A social history including parental input and observations of the student in his and her current educational environment should also be included in the evaluation. The school district has 60 calendar days to complete this evaluation.

- Once results are back, a multidisciplinary team (including the student's parents) should review the results and make a decision determining the student's eligibility for special education services under the guidelines of IDEA. If a student meets the criteria of one or more of the 13 disability categories, and the evaluation shows that the student needs special education and related services because of his or her disability, then the team will begin the process of implementing an **individualized education program (IEP).** If the student does not meet criteria, then the team or school may examine other ways to support the student, such as providing services under Section 504 of the Rehabilitation Act of 1973 (PL 93-112).

A leader needs to fully understand several key ideas of the eligibility process:

- Parent permission for evaluation
- Multidisciplinary evaluation required
    - Conducted in child's native language
    - Includes more than one measure
    - Completed within 60 days
- Multidisciplinary team (including parents) determine eligibility
- Next steps when a student is determined eligible or ineligible

In addition, several special considerations are specific to students with ASD in the decision of eligibility. First, it is important to clarify that a diagnosis of ASD is different from the eligibility category of autism in IDEA, which was added to the law in 1990 (prior to that time, students were not identified as having ASD using IDEA eligibility categories). ASD is a medical diagnosis that encompasses a wider range of individuals than those who fit IDEA's category of autism. IDEA defines *autism* as a developmental disability significantly affecting verbal and nonverbal communication and social interaction, generally evident before age 3, that adversely affects a child's educational performance. Engagement in repetitive activities and **stereotyped movements,** resistance to environmental change or change in daily routines, and unusual responses to sensory experiences are other characteristics often associated with autism. A student cannot be determined eligible under the category of autism if his or her educational performance is adversely affected primarily because the child has an emotional disturbance (34 C.F.R. § 300.8[c][1]).

Students sometimes receive a medical diagnosis of ASD outside of school, and parents may request that the student be evaluated for eligibility. The student's eligibility may or may not fit under the IDEA definition of autism. The eligibility category of autism defined in IDEA is most often applied to those students with more severe forms of autism as it appears on the spectrum. It is up to the multidisciplinary team, however, to make this determination. States sometimes vary in their interpretations of the IDEA disability definitions to make them broader. Thus, it is important to know your state's definition of autism when understanding eligibility decisions.

Students on the autism spectrum may be served in different ways because of the discrepancy between private ASD diagnoses and the IDEA eligibility label. The most important thing to ensure is that students with ASD receive the supports and services they need to be successful in school, regardless of their category of eligibility. If students with a private diagnosis of ASD do not fit the criteria of autism for a particular state, then they may be eligible for special education services under other categories of IDEA, including **developmental delay** or **other health impaired**. If students with ASD are not eligibile under the categories provided by IDEA, then they may be considered for a support plan under Section 504 of the Rehabilitation Act.

Free Appropriate Public Education

After a student is determined eligible under IDEA, that student is entitled to receive a FAPE, which is defined in IDEA as special education and related services that

> (a) are provided at public expense; (b) meet the standards of the state educational agency (SEA); (c) include an appropriate preschool, elementary, or secondary school education in the state involved; and (d) are provided in conformity with the individualized education program. (§ 1401[18][C])

The school district is responsible for providing the student's education as described in the IEP, which must be in effect at the beginning of the school year and be reviewed at least annually. IDEA requires that each student's IEP provide specialized instruction to address his or her unique learning needs. The law is clear about the depth and breadth of a student's IEP:

- Statements of present levels of academic and functional performance

- Measurable annual goals; some students may also require short-term objectives, depending on state requirements

- Statements of how a student's progress will be measured and reported
- Description of special education services, related services, and supplementary services based on **peer-reviewed research;** the IEP must also detail the duration and length of services, a start and end date, and the settings in which the services will be delivered
- If a student is not educated in general education, then a determination of the level of participation in general education must be provided, along with a rationale for that decision
- Description of classroom or testing adaptations or accommodations
- **Transition statements** or a transition plan should be included, depending on the age of the student

It is extremely important that the appropriate team of people collaborates to develop a student's IEP. According to IDEA, a student's IEP team must include the student's parents or guardians. Moreover, parents must play a meaningful role in the process. School-based members who must be on the IEP team include a representative of the school (usually a principal or assistant principal), a student's special education teacher and his or her general education teacher, a person who can explain the instructional implications of the evaluation, and other personnel deemed necessary to develop the student's special education program (e.g., school nurse, school psychologist, guidance counselor).

Yell, Katsiyannis, Ennis, and Losinski (2013) provided a useful discussion on errors frequently made in IEPs. They described the most frequent errors as procedural or substantive. **Procedural errors** are those situations in which school district personnel do not follow the federal requirements in developing an IEP, including

a. Failing to involve a student's parents in the IEP process
b. Predetermining a student's placement or program
c. Determining placement before having developed the IEP
d. Failing to field an appropriate IEP team
e. Failing to include all content requirements in the IEP (e.g., annual goals)
f. Failing to implement the IEP as written (Bateman, 2011; Yell, 2012; Yell et al., 2013)

Substantive errors are those processes that do not follow the federal requirements to create and implement an IEP that provides educational benefit, including failure to

a. Assess the student's academic and functional needs
b. Develop annual goals based on those needs
c. Write goals that are complete, appropriate, and measurable
d. Provide special education and related services that are effective and based on (EA) peer-reviewed research
e. Monitor the student's progress toward his or her goals and make instructional changes when necessary (Bateman, 2011; Yell, 2012; Yell et al., 2013)

Many of the questions that parents, administrators, teachers, and others have about IDEA's implementation have been asked and answered because it has been a law for decades. Answers to most questions can be found in the IDEA resource provided by the

U.S. Department of Education (http://www.doe.in.gov/sites/default/files/specialed/idea faq.pdf). This document is part of the U.S. Department of Education, Office of Special Education Programs web site (https://sites.ed.gov/idea). Individual states may have additional guidelines or requirements not listed on these federal web sites.

Least Restrictive Environment

IDEA requires that students with disabilities are educated with their typically developing peers to the maximum extent appropriate. Students in special education should only be removed to separate classes or schools when the nature or severity of their disabilities is such that they cannot receive an appropriate education in a general education classroom with supplementary aids and services (including resource room services). They should be educated in the LRE possible for meeting their needs.

LRE is an important consideration when determining a student's placement. A student's placement must be decided at least annually by a collaborative education team that includes the student's parent, and these people should be knowledgeable about the student, the meaning of the evaluation data, and the various placement options. The placement decision, which is not technically part of the IEP process, is usually made by a student's IEP team. The decision of where to place a student must follow development of the IEP and be based on the IEP.

Procedural Safeguards

IDEA mandates an extensive system of procedural safeguards to ensure that parents are equal participants in the special education process. The three primary safeguards include 1) notice and consent requirement, 2) **independent educational evaluations,** and 3) dispute resolution.

The notice requirements of IDEA state that school district personnel must provide notice to parents in a reasonable amount of time prior to the school's initiating, changing a student's identification, evaluation, or educational placement. Notice is also required if the school refuses to take action regarding the child's identification, evaluation, or educational placement. This requirement is referred to as ***prior written notice.*** The consent mandate requires that parental consent must be obtained prior to conducting a preplacement evaluation for eligibility and again prior to initial placement in a special education program.

Parents of a student with disabilities have a right to obtain an independent educational evaluation at public expense when they disagree with the educational evaluation conducted by school personnel. When parents ask for an independent educational evaluation, school personnel must supply them with information about where the independent educational evaluation may be obtained. When parents decide to have the evaluation done independently, the district must pay for the cost of the evaluation or see that it is provided at no cost to the parents. If, however, the school believes its evaluation was appropriate, then the school may initiate a due process hearing to prove that the evaluation was valid. Once an independent educational evaluation is conducted, including an independent evaluation at the parents' expense, school personnel must read and consider the results.

IDEA contains a formal dispute resolution process when parents and the school disagree about the identification, evaluation, placement, or the provision of a FAPE. A **due process hearing** and a **state complaint resolution process** are two dispute resolution routes. Parents or a school district may file a request for a hearing when due process occurs. A school district must offer **mediation** in which a trained and impartial mediator will attempt to facilitate a settlement between the parties. If this is unsuccessful, or if the parents refuse mediation, then either party may file for a due process hearing. A resolution meeting must be held prior to the hearing to attempt to solve the dispute. If the resolution process is unsuccessful, then the due process hearing will be held. An impartial due process hearing office presides over the hearing, and any party in the hearing has the right to be represented by counsel, present evidence, compel the attendance of witnesses, examine and cross-examine witnesses, obtain a written or electronic verbatim record of the hearing, and be provided with the written findings of fact by the hearing officer. The hearing officer announces the decision once the hearing ends, and it is binding on both parties. If the hearing office finds against the school district, then he or she may order certain remedies be implemented (e.g., tuition reimbursement, compensatory education). Either party may appeal the hearing officer's decision to state or federal court.

Filing a complaint with the **state educational agency (SEA)** is the other route to dispute resolution. A parent may file a state complaint that a school district has violated IDEA within 1 year of the occurrence of the violation. Parents must notify the school district that they are filing a complaint with the SEA. Complaints can be filed on any issues involving identification, evaluation, placement, or programming. The state then has 60 days to investigate the complaint and compose a written ruling on its decision. The written decision must 1) address each allegation in the complaint, 2) detail the state's findings of fact and conclusions, and 3) provide the reasoning behind the decision. IDEA grants SEAs broad discretion in awarding remedies in cases of IDEA violations.

EVERY STUDENT SUCCEEDS ACT, NO CHILD LEFT BEHIND ACT, AND ELEMENTARY AND SECONDARY EDUCATION ACT

The **Every Student Succeeds Act (ESSA) of 2015** (PL 114-95), formerly known as the No Child Left Behind (NCLB) Act of 2001 (PL 107-110) and the Elementary and Secondary Education Act of 1965 (PL 89-10), contain provisions that directly affect students with ASD. Even though the ESSA is legislation that primarily focuses on students in the general education setting (as did NCLB), students with disabilities are a vital part of the K–12 system and are thereby covered by this new legislation. The ESSA includes provisions that will help ensure the success of all students, including students with ASD, and schools by 1) upholding critical protections for students who have high needs and are disadvantaged; 2) requiring all students be taught to high academic **standards** that will prepare them to succeed in college and careers; 3) providing vital information (via statewide assessments) regarding student progress to educators, families, students, and communities; 4) including evidence-based and place-based interventions; 5) increasing access to high-quality preschool, and 6) maintaining accountability to affect positive change in the lowest performing schools (U.S. Department of Education, 2017a). In addition, the ESSA narrows the role of federal government by requiring each state to submit a flexible consolidated education plan that addresses academic standards, assessment, and accountability (Darrow, 2016); these items build on the previous provisions contained in the NCLB revision of the Elementary and Secondary Education Act. It is imperative to look at NCLB because the U.S. Secretary of Education has implemented and released the updated template for the consolidated state plans (U.S. Department of Education, 2017b).

The original purpose of NCLB was to ensure that students enrolled in public school systems were being taught by well-qualified instructors and were achieving at a level that indicated proficiency across academic areas. This was to take place in a safe, drug-free environment. This legislation included several components (i.e., accountability, highly qualified personnel, implementing scientifically based instruction) that have affected how schools provide educational services to all students, including those with ASD and other disabilities. These components affect individuals with ASD being served in public schools. Yell, Drasgow, and Lowrey (2005) provided a comprehensive discussion of NCLB and students with ASD.

First, the provisions of accountability for school systems directly affected individuals with ASD. Although states varied in their implementation of NCLB, individuals with ASD were included in statewide standardized assessment. This assessment may have been the general assessment used for all students, a modified assessment, or an alternate assessment. The test scores of these students were included in each school district's annual progress measures.

NCLB also required the employment of highly qualified personnel to work with students. Students with ASD had to be served by teachers and paraprofessionals that met each state's definition of highly qualified. It is important to understand how the definition of highly qualified was applied to teachers and paraprofessionals assigned to deliver instruction and support students with ASD.

Finally, NCLB required the implementation of scientifically based instruction, which has been one of the most explored areas for students with ASD since the passage of NCLB. Scientifically based instruction involves instructional practices that are supported by rigorous research. The research must demonstrate that these instructional practices are effective for the content area and the population receiving instruction. There are several ways to easily identify those educational methods and strategies that are based on evidence from research (see Chapter 3 for a comprehensive discussion of evidence-based practices).

Overall, NCLB defined educational practices and procedures that directly affected how individuals with ASD were taught and how their annual progress was monitored. In addition, NCLB provided guidelines on who is appropriate to teach or support individuals with ASD. It is important for leaders to understand the application of this legislation to individuals with disabilities, including those with ASD. Yell and Drasgow (2005) described the implications of NCLB for personnel working with students with disabilities:

- Know the law
- Assess students for instruction
- Use instructional procedures grounded in scientifically based research
- Collect meaningful data on student progress

Educational leaders who follow these steps can ensure students with ASD receive an appropriate education as defined by NCLB and, soon to follow, ESSA.

Many questions and answers have been asked and answered about NCLB because it has been a law since 2001. An NCLB question-and-answer resource is provided by the U.S. Department of Education (http://www2.ed.gov/nclb/overview/intro/faqs.html). Individual states may have additional guidelines or requirements not listed on this federal web site.

States are seeking approval for their ESSA plans as this is being written. The NCLB guidelines can be used until your state's ESSA plan is in place. At that time, you should carefully review your state's ESSA plan for any changes in the provisions not mentioned above.

SECTION 504 OF THE REHABILITATION ACT AND THE AMERICANS WITH DISABILITIES ACT

Section 504 of the Rehabilitation Act is a civil rights law protecting individuals with disabilities from discrimination in public facilities and services funded by federal dollars. The **Americans with Disabilities Act** (ADA) of 1990 (PL 101-336) extended those protections to privately owned facilities and services. Section 504 and the ADA work together to protect people with disabilities against discrimination based on a person's disability in all settings, including school systems. Both are overseen by the Office of Civil Rights in the U.S. Department of Education. These laws are similar to other civil rights laws that extend protection against discrimination on the basis of race, color, and national origin (Title VII of the Civil Rights Act of 1964 [PL 88-352]) and sex (Title IX of the Education Amendments of 1972 [PL 92-318, 86 Stat. 235]).

Regulations to Section 504 contain educational rights for students with disabilities. The education provided to students with disabilities must be equivalent to the education provided to students without disabilities. This is the FAPE requirement under Section 504. Unlike IDEA, a disability under 504 is more loosely defined as a physical or mental impairment that substantially limits a **major life activity,** including caring for one's self, walking, seeing, speaking, breathing, working, learning, and performing manual tasks (34 C.F.R. 104.3[j][2][ii]).

Students with ASD are protected under IDEA and Section 504. In almost all cases, students who are eligible to receive services under IDEA are doubly covered under Section 504. Special education services for students who are covered by both laws are generally provided under IDEA, which is the more specific of the two laws in terms of educational rights and obligations. Students covered by IDEA, however, are always protected from discrimination under Section 504. If students with ASD do not meet the eligibility requirements of IDEA, then they can receive educational services under Section 504. A **Section 504 accommodation plan** can be developed and implemented to ensure these students receive the appropriate supports and services necessary to support their participation and achievement in education.

Accommodation plans may look different from state to state and district to district because the regulations for Section 504 are not as detailed as those for IDEA. How those plans are created, managed, and updated may also vary. All school districts are required to have Section 504 coordinators, however. Leaders need to identify the 504 procedures for their district and know the requirements of the law. A question-and-answer guide is offered by the U.S. Department of Education (http://www2.ed.gov/about/offices/list/ocr/504faq.html), and it serves as a useful resource to understand the relationship of IDEA and 504 as well as the provisions of Section 504.

CASE LAW

Several important cases have been decided since 2004 regarding the education of students with ASD. Selected cases are briefly described here based on specific themes. As has been historically demonstrated in the past, these court decisions may influence the language used to clarify provisions in the next authorization of IDEA.

The landscape of case law changes quickly. ASD is the most litigated area by disability category (Zirkel, 2002, 2011), so it is important that leaders supporting students with ASD stay abreast of current decisions in the courts and consider how they might affect schoolwide practices and individual programming. Planning for systematic changes is always more prudent than having to scrap a system and begin again. Please see the Resources section at the end of this chapter for web sites with up-to-date information.

Free Appropriate Public Education

Students with disabilities are guaranteed a FAPE that confers meaningful educational benefit. Each component of this key principle (free, appropriate, public, education) has been examined via case law. Some general cases have explored the concept of FAPE (*Bd. Of Education v. Rowley,* 1982), and several important cases explore the concept of FAPE as it relates specifically to the education of students with ASD. Methods used for instruction are included under the concept of FAPE. The following cases looked at how the implementation of certain instructional methodologies affected a FAPE for students with ASD. The school district in *County School Board of Henrico County VA v. R. T. et al.* (2006) was hoping for a reversal of an earlier ruling in favor of the parents. R.T.'s parents initially filed suit, claiming that Henrico County was not providing a FAPE to R.T., their son with ASD. The primary issue in this case was that R.T. was not making adequate progress under the instructional methodology used by the school district (i.e., Treatment and Education of Autistic and related Communication Handicapped Children [TEACCH]). IEP goals and objectives were carried over multiple IEPs across several years without achievement. The parents used applied behavior analysis (ABA) therapy at home, and R.T. made substantial progress. This instructional methodology was rejected by the IEP team for school implementation. At issue was that R.T.'s primary instructional need was to learn basic **attending skills**, and TEACCH did not address that need. The parents won in the original suit as well as in this case based on the court's decision that the student was not receiving educational benefit from Henrico's programming and instruction. Several other cases brought to court by the parents of students with ASD have been decided regarding implementing ABA over other instructional methodologies, including *Bucks County Department of Mental Health/Mental Retardation* (2004), *Appellant v. Commonwealth of Pennsylvania, Department of Public Welfare* (2004), *Zachary Deal v. Hamilton Bd. of Ed.* (2004, 2008), and *L.B. and J.B. on Behalf of K.B. v. Nebo Sch. Dist. et al.* (2004). Findings from these cases demonstrate that school systems must provide the most appropriate instructional supports and services to meet each student's unique learning needs, and they must create an educational environment in which the child demonstrates progress on and achievement of learning goals and objectives. These findings have important implications for leaders helping to guide educational programming for students with ASD. They emphasize the importance of supporting teachers to design instruction and a classroom environment that promote students' success and progress—both are important in providing a FAPE.

Placement

Placement is an additional area of litigation to consider. Although some of the previously mentioned cases affirmed private placement when appropriate instruction was not being utilized in public settings, cases also provide additional clarity for placement within the IEP process. For example, *A.K. v. Alexandria City School Board* (2007) identified a procedural error in IEP development. The parents of A.K. were verbally offered several day school placements for consideration during the IEP meeting, but they were not noted on the IEP. The court found that A.K. was not denied a FAPE, but placements under consideration should be noted in writing on the IEP.

In addition, the concept of LRE is often examined under the issue of placement. Parents in the following cases sought recompense for their child's placement in a more restrictive environment: *Corpus Christi Indep. Sch. Dist. v. Christopher N.* (2012), *W.S. v. Rye City Sch. Dist.* (2006), and *M.S. Ex. Rel. Simchick v. Fairfax County Sch. Bd.* (2009). The school district won in each of these cases as long as they could demonstrate they were providing or proposing services that would ensure a FAPE. There are also cases supporting a school district's desire to move students to a more restrictive placement when parents may desire a more inclusive placement. School districts in each of these cases, however, demonstrated that a more restrictive environment was educationally necessary to meet the unique needs of the child and an LRE could not adequately meet those needs. Examples of cases demonstrating this are *Las Virgenes Unif. Sch. Dist. v. S.K.* (2010), *E.G. v. City School District of New Rochelle* (2009), and *S.K. v. Parsippany-Troy Hills Bd. of Educ.* (2008). Although the student's more restrictive placement was upheld in all the cases, students were still placed in general education classes and had experiences with their peers for part of their day.

The U.S. Supreme Court ruled in *Endrew v. Douglas County School District* (2017) that schools must offer IEPs that are 1) reasonably calculated to enable a child to make appropriate progress considering the child's circumstances (e.g., specifically designed to meet a child's unique needs) and 2) not a form document. Endrew is a boy with ASD who was initially receiving his education in the local public school system. Endrew's parents ultimately decided to enroll him in a private specialized school where he eventually made significant academic and social gains due to two reasons: 1) Endrew's academic progress seemed to stall, and 2) they were issued two versions of a new IEP that resembled his previous IEPs, even though Endrew's progress seemed to plateau. The U.S. Supreme Court unanimously voted to vacate the 10th circuit court's decision and remanded the decision back to the 10th circuit court to reconsider their prevision decision in light of the Supreme Court's new standard, which is that IEPs must be reasonably calculated to enable a student to make progress in light of his or her circumstances.

Extended School Year Services

A school district's failure to consider **extended school year (ESY) services** can be considered a denial of FAPE (*Bend Lapine Sch. Dist. v. K.H.*, 2005). It is important that ESY services not only examine **regression and recoupment** (*Bend Lapine Sch. Dist. v. K.H.*, 2005) but also use a multifactored approach as defined in *Johnson v. Independent School* (1990). In addition, general school programs, such as summer camps, may not be appropriate to meet students' unique needs (Foxborough Reg. Charter Sch., 2006).

Although legislation and case law does provide a way to measure minimal compliance in services, the spirit of the law ensures that school systems maximize services for each individual. Legislation is intended to create guidelines for practice. Leaders can always do more than the law suggests, but they should never do less.

ADDITIONAL RESOURCES

Web Sites

- LRP Education Administration and Law
  http://www.lrp.com/ed.html
    LRP exclusively represents school districts. A free 30-day trial is offered for their Special Education Connection, which includes case law, federal statutes and regulations, tools, and strategies.

- U.S. Department of Education IDEA
  https://sites.ed.gov/idea
- U.S. Department of Education IDEA Frequently Asked Questions
  http://www.doe.in.gov/sites/default/files/specialed/ideafaq.pdf
- U.S. Department of Education NCLB Question and Answer
  http://www2.ed.gov/nclb/overview/intro/faqs.html
- Wrightslaw
  http://www.wrightslaw.com/info/autism.index.htm
  A free legal advocacy web resource offering up-to-date summaries of legislation and case law. They offer a specific section on ASD. Signing up for their newsletter, visiting this site occasionally, or attending a training is a good way to stay up to date on the latest case law in ASD.

REFLECTION QUESTIONS

1. Sarah Jackson, the new superintendent, meets with the district principals and notes multiple instances of school leaders referencing provisions of NCLB. As the conversation continues, Dr. Jackson realizes she needs to lead an informative discussion regarding the ESSA. Compare and contrast the ESSA and NCLB to help Dr. Jackson disseminate the most important information of the ESSA to her building administrators. What are the most important provisions of the ESSA? What NCLB provisions were expanded on in the ESSA? What new provisions of the ESSA were not present in NCLB?

2. Jason Gray is attending his first meeting as a school principal after successfully completing his master's degree in education in school administration. The district superintendent begins the meeting by focusing on the district's current Child Find program. He notes the progress of the program but states, "A lot of work needs to be done." He asks for volunteers to help with this initiative. Jason, wanting to prove his worth as an administrator, offers to help. After receiving the positive affirmation that he sought (a verbal "thank you" from his boss), Jason begins to catalog the information he needs to address. Make a list of activities that can be implemented as part of a successful Child Find program to help Jason. Begin by explaining the role of a Child Find program and its relationship to the zero reject principle of IDEA.

3. Amanda Johnson has landed the responsibility of overseeing the drafting of all the district special education IEPs as part of her new job as Director of Curriculum and Instruction (and due to her special education background). Ms. Johnson intends on drafting a memorandum for all special education teachers. Help Ms. Johnson create this memorandum by listing 1) pertinent information that should be included in every IEP and 2) the two types of errors most frequently made when creating IEPs. In addition, describe any new legal cases that affect the writing of IEPs.

4. It is October, and Jared Douglas, the high school principal, reflects on a somewhat uneventful first month of school. Someone knocking on his door draws his attention back to the present. Once he answers, a mother he is vaguely familiar with begins to speak in a rushed fashion. "Here it is. Proof. My son Adam has autism. Dr. Pearson just diagnosed him. I want Adam to receive special education services starting tomorrow. I know the law. That's our right." Jared is a bit taken aback. He wants to not only calm but also educate the parent. Help Jared formulate a response that will 1) tactfully inform the parent of the special education referral process and 2) explain the differentiation between a diagnosis of autism and eligibility for special education services under the category of autism in IDEA.

5. Dr. Wendy Wilson, a specialized autism consultant, has been asked to lead a districtwide faculty development meeting attended by all school personnel. Dr. Wilson decides to begin the meeting by explaining the current regulations that affect students with ASD. Help Dr. Wilson complete this task by listing and explaining the primary provisions of the current federal legislation, regulations, and case law that most directly affect students with ASD.

6. The tension in the room is quite apparent. It has been 2 hours since the IEP meeting began, and the two sides (i.e., parents, school representatives) are no closer to reaching an agreement now than they were at the beginning of the meeting. Mrs. Adams, the district director of special education, realizes they are at an impasse and intends to inform the parents of their rights. Help Mrs. Adams by listing and fully explaining the three primary procedural safeguards of IDEA using clear and easy-to-understand language.

3. Evidence-Based Practices for Students With ASD

How Will I Know It When I See It?

K. Alisa Lowrey and Christina R. Carnahan

> **QUESTIONS THIS CHAPTER WILL ANSWER**
>
> 1. What is an evidence-based practice?
> 2. What are the evidence-based practices for students with ASD?
> 3. How will I know an evidence-based practice when I see one?
> 4. What are the Council for Exceptional Children standards for teaching students with ASD, and why do they matter?

WHAT ARE EVIDENCE-BASED PRACTICES?

Evidence-based practices can be instrumental in intervention planning for students with ASD and are critical to consider when designing a supportive learning environment. It is important to understand exactly what evidence-based practices are, how they are determined, and how to measure them when they are being implemented correctly. *Evidence-based practices* have been defined as "instructional techniques with meaningful research support that represent critical tools in bridging the research-to-practice gap and improving student outcomes" (Cook & Cook, 2011, p. 2). Evidence-based practices are supported by research and are determined through careful measurement and consideration of the following four areas—research design, quality of supporting research studies, quantity of research studies, and the **efficacy** of the supporting studies (Cook & Cook, 2013). The term *evidence-based practice* is used to refer to the science of teaching—science that has been designed correctly, implemented correctly (i.e., with fidelity), implemented frequently enough to show replicability, and shown to be effective.

The term *evidence-based practice* has been used synonymously and incorrectly with the terms *best practice, recommended practice,* and **research-based practice** (Cook & Cook, 2013). These terms indicate different measures of educational practice. Evidence-based practices have established efficacy (i.e., produced the intended result) that is demonstrated through peer-reviewed research and meet one of the following criteria: 1) two high-quality experimental or quasi-experimental group design studies; 2) five high-quality single-subject design studies, conducted by three different researchers or research groups; and 3) one high-quality randomized or quasi-experimental group design study and three high-quality single-subject design studies conducted by at least three different investigators or research groups (across the group and single-subject design studies) (Mundy & Mastergeorge, 2012; Simpson, 2005). Evidence-based practices meet very specific standards in terms of the quality, quantity, and design of the supporting research. In contrast, the terms *best* and *recommended practice* have no agreed-on criteria and may be promoted regardless of the level of empirical evidence to support their use (Cook & Cook, 2013). *Research-based practice* can be used broadly to describe a practice that has been supported by research findings (Cook & Cook, 2013; Cook, Tankersley, & Landrum, 2013), or it may be used to describe a practice equal to or more rigorous than evidence-based practice, as described in NCLB. Additional confusion often stems from other ways researchers describe practices for students with ASD. Simpson (2005) defined ***promising practices*** or *developing practices* as those practices demonstrating efficacy and utility for individuals with ASD but not at the level of an evidence-based practice. Promising or developing practices need additional study to verify efficacy and utility before it can be verified as an evidence-based practice.

Confusion about terminology in education has led to misuse and distrust of terms such as *evidence-based practice, research-based practice,* and *best practice*. National centers have been established in education that help navigate these terms. The National Professional Development Center (NPDC), specifically in Wong et al. (2015) and on the AFIRM (Autism Focused Intervention Resources and Modules) web site (http://afirm.fpg.unc.edu/afirm-modules), utilizes the term *evidence-based practices* to delineate practices found to be effective for the instruction of students with ASD.

One of the core missions of the National Autism Center (NAC), which is housed at the May Institute, is to disseminate evidence-based information supporting the effective treatment of individuals with ASD (http://www.nationalautismcenter.org/national-standards-project). The NAC expands the definition of *evidence-based practices* to include "the use of professional judgment, consideration of client and family values and preferences, and knowledge and understanding of the best research evidence" (http://www.nationalautismcenter.org/national-standards-project/phase-2/what-makes-phase-ii-unique).

It is important to communicate (i.e., sharing and helping to translate) information about these evidence-based practices with educators and families. Teams, including professional and families, often need support to determine how these practices might work in a specific setting or for a specific learner. A leader should understand the term *evidence-based practices,* the stringent criteria this term refers to, and how to communicate the importance of evidence-based practices to the educators that teach students with ASD on a daily basis.

The NPDC used a rigorous process to vet instructional strategies and ultimately develop a thorough list of evidence-based practices that meet the research criteria described earlier (see Wong et al., 2015). Currently, 27 evidence-based practices have been identified by the NPDC for instructing individuals with ASD (Wong et al., 2015). Not only did Wong and colleagues delineate the practices that meet the stringent evidence-based practice criteria, but they also correlated these with the age of learner with whom the practice has been tested.

The NAC completed a two-phase analysis to determine the most effective interventions. Phase 1 covers published educational and behavioral research from 1957 to 2007. Phase 2 provides updates and includes findings for interventions applied with individuals age 22 and older. Criteria for inclusion/exclusion, specific intervention targets, ages of participants, and diagnostic groups are provided. The NAC reviews included additional treatments and therapies excluded from the NPDC reviews. Additional information about evidence-based practices is presented in the next section.

EVIDENCE-BASED PRACTICES FOR STUDENTS WITH ASD

Identifying Evidence-Based Practices

Understanding evidence-based practices is an essential first step in cultivating high-quality instructional environments for learners with ASD. Equally important is understanding resources and strategies for identifying and evaluating the utility of specific evidence-based practices for individual learners and specific classroom settings. Although this process may be somewhat challenging, both the NPDC and the NAC translated the scientific evidence behind instructional strategies into lists. As previously mentioned, the NAC report includes 14 general categories of practice, often combining specific strategies into a larger group. For example, **reinforcement** would fit into the category of behavioral interventions. The NPDC lists 27 practices that have effectively been used in classrooms, and it is an easy list to guide educational decision making. Yet, both reports are important and beneficial for educators. It is particularly important that two separate agencies conducted rigorous examinations of practice commonly used to support students with ASD and arrived at similar findings. Table 3.1 contains a list of current evidence-based practices for students with ASD.

Table 3.1. Evidence-based practices effective for individuals with ASD

Evidence-based practice	Definition
Antecedent-based intervention	Planning events or circumstances that come before the incidence of a behavior. It is thought to reduce said behavior.
Cognitive behavioral intervention	Teaching the organization of thinking processes that cause alterations in an overt behavior.
Differential reinforcement of alternative, incompatible, or other behavior	Delivery of positive penalties for behaviors or absence of behaviors that reduce an undesirable behavior. Reinforcement should be provided when 1) the student is performing a behavior that is desirable, 2) the student is performing a behavior that cannot be done alongside the undesirable behavior, and 3) the student is not involving him- or herself in the undesirable behavior.
Discrete trial teaching	Involves one teacher and one student in the hopes to teach the desirable behavior. Typically consists of trials that consider the teacher's presentation, the student's response to that presentation, a positive penalty, and a pause prior to moving forward with the next set of instructions.
Exercise	Exercising to decrease challenging behaviors and increase desired behaviors.
Extinction	Not providing positive reinforcers to decrease the undesired behavior.
Functional behavioral assessment	Evaluating information regarding an undesired behavior. It is designed to define the behavior, give an idea of preceding or following events that could have caused the behavior, and discover the meaning of the behavior.

(continued)

Table 3.1. *(continued)*

Evidence-based practice	Definition
Functional communication training	An attempt to replace undesired behavior with a more communicative desired behavior that will serve the same means.
Modeling	Showing the learner how the desired behavior is to be performed in hopes of eventually having the learner perform the desired behavior without the model.
Naturalistic intervention	Involvement strategies that are in the learners' setting and place of comfort, including specific routines, settings, or activities. Teachers can see how learners absorb information in their comfort zones and figure out how to apply that to their teaching.
Parent-implemented intervention	Parents get involved at home and work side by side with their children to make sure their maximum amount of skills are being presented or their undesired behaviors are decreasing.
Peer-mediated instruction and intervention	Students with ASD interact with typically developing students to increase desired social behaviors. Teachers will often teach the typically developing students strategies to help with this.
Picture Exchange Communication System	Students are told to show a picture of something that they desire to the communication partners with whom they are working. There are six phases—how to communicate, distance and persistence, picture discrimination, sentence structure, responsive requesting, and commenting.
Pivotal response training	Key learning strategies such as motivation and self-imitation are presented in settings that are comfortable to the student.
Prompting	Cues such as verbal, gestural, or physical are given to students to help them perform a desired behavior.
Reinforcement	A positive notion after a student performs the desired behavior to get him or her to perform the behavior in the future.
Response interruption/redirection	Interrupting the student's undesired behavior to distract and sidetrack him or her from the undesired behavior.
Scripting	A repeatedly practiced description of a particular behavior that can be verbal or written.
Self-management	Students determine whether their behavior is appropriate and, if it is appropriate, then reward themselves in a positive regard.
Social narratives	These narratives are individualized to each student's needs, define social situations, and provide some cues for conversations.
Social skills training	Group or individual teaching of how students with ASD should interact with all types of people they may encounter, including role-playing and feedback from teachers or peers that can help the student with ASD.
Structured play group	A planned, well-thought-out play group involving peers and role play to improve the social skills of students with ASD.
Task analysis	Breaking down a task into small steps to better learn the task. Video modeling and positive reinforcement are often used.
Technology-aided instruction and intervention	Technology-based learning to better benefit the student with ASD.
Time delay	A delay in time from the moment a skill is presented to the student to when he or she is to respond. This is used to have a desired outcome from the student without help from the teacher or peers.
Video modeling	A recording of the desired behavior in video model form.
Visual support	Any visual forms of representation that will enhance the learner's outcome.

From Wong, C., et al. (2015). Evidence-based practices for children, youth, and young adults with autism spectrum disorder: A comprehensive review. *Journal of Autism and Developmental Disorders, 45*(7), 1951–1966; adapted by permission.

Implementing Evidence-Based Practices

After identifying evidence-based practices, the next step is focusing on effectively integrating these practices in educational settings. The NPDC developed a set of comprehensive models that serve as a valuable tool for translating research into practice (i.e., AFIRM; http://afirm.fpg.unc.edu). Each module includes a description of the specific practice, a rationale, and detailed directions for planning and case scenarios. The modules also include links to a practice brief, or general summary describing the step-by-step outline of instructions for implementation; checklist to be used during implementation; and a review of scientific research by which this practice was determined to be evidence based. In addition, the AFIRM site offers a module on selecting evidence-based practices, including strategies for identifying specific targets, setting goals, and implementing the intervention. This is a free resource that is useful for educators and families. The modules and briefs may be valuable in crafting professional development for individual teachers and professionals, specific teams, or schoolwide.

The NAC also created several valuable tools to support teams in implementing evidence-based practices, including online and print-based resources for educators and families. The print-based resources include several texts for educators and parents that address the implementation of evidence-based practices in schools. These books are free when accessed online. The online resources include a brief list of the practices, information regarding the characteristics of ASD, and Autism: Closer Look (http://www.nationalautismcenter.org/resources/autism-a-closer-look), with specific suggestions and strategies related to topics of interest to a variety of stakeholders, including teachers and families.

The Autism Internet Modules (http://www.autisminternetmodules.org) are another valuable resource to support school teams in translating research to practice. The Autism Internet Modules offer clear descriptions of some specific practices, including the research base, and include a model demonstration of the practice, often supplemented with videos or visual examples of instructional procedures, materials, and assessments. In addition, activities and quizzes are included to inform individualized professional development. Finally, the National Autism Association (http://nationalautismassociation.org) and Autism Speaks (https://www.autismspeaks.org) are two organizations that offer a variety of resources introducing the characteristics of ASD and some evidence-based practices. Other resources can help leaders and school teams recognize and implement evidence-based practices for students with ASD and are readily available for anyone to use. A list of resources is included at the end of this chapter.

An initial time commitment may be necessary for leaders to gain an understanding of the various evidence-based practices, especially if these practices might only benefit a few students in the school. Many of these evidence-based practices show effectiveness for use with other learning needs, however, not only with students with ASD or students with disabilities. Learning about the practices that have been effective for students with ASD increases leaders' knowledge of practices that may be effective for a diverse population of learners. Decisions on how to support individual learners become clearer and more concrete when teams allow evidence-based practices to guide their instruction. Creating a professional community of learners who study the science of their profession and learn to correctly implement these practices leads to better outcomes for students in the school, district, and state. Using evidence-based practices does not need to be a mysterious or unachievable goal—there are concrete strategies for effectively implementing these strategies and being able to recognize them in action in school. How will an educator know when an evidence-based practice is being used in a classroom? The next section answers this question.

EVIDENCE-BASED PRACTICES: HOW WILL EDUCATORS KNOW THEM WHEN THEY SEE THEM?

Evidence-based practices share several common characteristics. They are specific **pedagogical** techniques supported by scientific evidence of effectiveness when implemented with fidelity. The following common characteristics will help educators recognize them.

First, all evidence-based practices are specific, named interventions that have been tested through peer-reviewed, validated research (Cook & Cook, 2013). They are not happenstance or one teacher's special way of doing things, but they are established practices that have been tested and retested in educational settings with students with ASD and other disabilities to demonstrate effectiveness.

Second, all evidence-based practices have specific procedures for implementation. These procedures may be more student directed and linked to students' interest and natural behaviors, such as **naturalistic interventions** (Schreibman et al., 2015), which unfold within the context of natural interactions or daily routines and capitalize on the students' interests and preferences. Other evidence-based practices are more structured and depend heavily on teacher direction (e.g., **discrete trial training**) (Schreibman et al., 2015). All evidence-based practices for students with ASD have outlined procedures to be followed, regardless of the directional framework. The instructional modules highlighted in the previous section provide evidence-based practices procedures in detail. These procedures should be part of a teacher's lesson plan and can be shared with paraprofessionals, peers, parents, and others for implementation. Each practice should be implemented with **fidelity**, which means that the person implementing each intervention should follow standardized protocols that have demonstrated effectiveness. It is not enough for a teacher to do part of the recommended procedures—if only part of the procedure is followed, then there is no fidelity in the intervention and the practice no longer qualifies as evidence based. For example, a teacher may claim to be using a **time delay** intervention, yet not honor the proposed delay or may be repeating a prompt, which invalidates the procedure. Fidelity of implementation is a critical component to maintaining evidence-based practices. None of these interventions are appropriate or effective if done haphazardly. It is not enough to know the names of evidence-based practices and follow some of the components; teachers must also understand the procedures and follow them as recommended and validated by research.

Third, all these procedures include a measurement of effectiveness. Analysis of data is the only way one can truly know if students are making progress (Salvia, Ysseldyke, & Bolt, 2012). If students are making progress when an intervention is in place, then that intervention may be effective. If students do not make progress when an intervention is in place, then the intervention may be ineffective. Data collection and analysis for educational decision making, otherwise known as **progress monitoring,** is key to each of these evidence-based practices. It is not enough to conduct these evidence-based practices with fidelity of implementation. One must also collect data on student progress and make decisions about the effectiveness of the intervention based on that data. If data do not demonstrate student progress, then individualized adjustments should be made to the intervention. If data continue to show no progress, then a change in intervention should be made.

Finally, all these interventions require planning prior to implementation. None of these evidence-based practices should be implemented "on the fly" while in the process of teaching. Preplanning these instructional interventions for appropriate implementation and measurement is critical to maintaining the efficacy of each of these practices. The teacher should have procedures to which he or she can refer and data collection sheets or supports to use during sessions, and he or she should prepare the materials ahead of time. If this element of preparation is missing, then he or she is not appropriately using the evidence-based practice.

Educators can look at these indicators and monitor the implementation of these practices to determine if evidence-based practices are in use. They can also discuss the guidelines for implementing evidence-based practices with their teachers to be sure they understand how to make these interventions a reality in their classrooms. Ensuring teacher effectiveness in instructing students with ASD is one of the key responsibilities as a school leader.

Leaders often ask for strategies that can support increased use of evidence-based practices with fidelity in their schools. Approaches vary from comprehensive, schoolwide efforts, to those targeting specific classrooms or even students. Collaborative approaches are discussed in Chapter 5, but the following are a few points for consideration. First, consider a distributed leadership model (Mangin, 2007) in which a small group of individuals, rather than just one school leader, are tasked with researching the 27 evidence-based practices. Second, encourage educators to use the national coordinating centers previously mentioned as guidelines for gaining access to professional development. Third, encourage educators to use the Evidence-Based Practice Classroom Observation Tool, which is described in detail in Chapter 4, to identify the evidence-based practices they already use and build on these over time. The following case example highlights how one leader applied these guidelines.

Mrs. George is the vice principal in charge of special education at Sanders Middle School. Mrs. George works with seven special education teachers that support students with ASD and other developmental disorders. Mr. Snow, a recently hired teacher, is already teaching a group of six students with ASD in third through fifth grade while working on certification in special education. Teachers submit budgetary requests for professional development prior to the beginning of school. Mrs. George reviews these requests and sees that Mr. Snow has requested substantial funding to attend a professional development training on facilitated communication strategies. Mr. Snow has included a rationale that states facilitated communication is an accepted strategy for students with ASD. He also states he could attend the training and share the professional development with the other teachers. Although this collaborative attitude is great, Mrs. George is not sure about this strategy because she is not a special educator. She has never heard of facilitated communication and thinks she should make sure this is a legitimate practice before signing approval to fund this professional development. Mrs. George remembers she has bookmarked the NPDC web site on her computer. She looks through the list of evidence-based practices and does not find facilitated communication listed. She scans through those practices listed with some support and still does not see facilitated communication. Just to be sure, she looks it up on the NAC site as well. It is listed as having an unestablished level of evidence. Mrs. George decides it is not wise to support professional development on a practice that is not known to be effective in supporting students with ASD. She responds to Mr. Snow's request and includes the links for the NPDC and the NAC web sites. She shares that her school will support additional learning on any of the evidence-based practices listed.

Mrs. George implements a collaborative planning approach to professional development the next spring and schedules a meeting with the seven teachers. The teachers decide together to investigate the NAC report and the NPDC and determine specific areas for development. After doing some reading, the team determines they need additional information about several practices, including 1) video modeling, 2) peer-mediated instruction, and 3) social skills training. The team meets a few weeks later with Mrs. George and reports on their targeted needs, including resources available online and in their state. They were able to gather a good deal of information regarding video modeling through the available online resources. They also gathered a lot of valuable information online regarding peer-mediated instruction and social skills training, but they hoped to attend a series of workshops around their state. Three teachers expressed interest in peer-mediated instruction and four in social skills training. Mrs. George and her teachers decided the group would divide and conquer. After attending the workshops, they would discuss the information and share the essential components at faculty meetings the following school year.

PROFESSIONAL STANDARDS FOR TEACHERS: PREPARING EDUCATORS TO SUPPORT STUDENTS WITH DISABILITIES

The Council for Exceptional Children (CEC) is the premiere professional organization committed to ensuring the success of learners with disabilities and the professionalism and skilled performance of those who support them in their education. Establishing professional standards for practicing teachers has been a prioritized goal for CEC since 1922. Teacher preparation programs use the CEC professional standards of practice in preparation of future teachers. These standards exist to guide teachers in the ethical instruction of students with ASD and other disabilities. The CEC has developed a set of standards for those teachers who work with students with developmental disabilities and ASD. Initial and advanced sets of standards are available to guide educators' practice and to aid leaders in identifying the types of skills and behaviors that professionals working with these students should possess (https://www.cec.sped.org/Standards/Special-Educator-Professional-Preparation-Standards/CEC-Initial-and-Advanced-Specialty-Sets; https://www.cec.sped.org/Standards/Ethical-Principles-and-Practice-Standards). Leaders who may not be trained in special education and teaching students with specific disabilities can gain access to these standards to more clearly understand the skills that teachers within these areas should demonstrate with proficiency. Examples of the skills include designing evidence-based, systematic instruction that is individualized to meet the needs of the student; using frequent measures of student progress; creating structured environments to support learning; using evidence-based behavioral strategies to assess, teach, and replace challenging behaviors; and teaching communication and social skills.

Evidence-based practices are the science that teachers need to know to be effective. Creating opportunities in which special education teachers trained in these practices can share, demonstrate, and teach others how to effectively practice interventions and provide supports for students with ASD is an additional way to ensure quality programming and a supportive environment for professionals.

ADDITIONAL RESOURCES

Web Sites

- Autism Focused Intervention Modules (AFIRM)
  http://afirm.fpg.unc.edu/afirm-modules
- Autism Internet Modules (on EBP)
  http://www.autisminternetmodules.org
- Autism Speaks Professional Development Resources
  https://www.autismspeaks.org/science/professional-development-resources
- CEEDAR Evidence-Based Practices for Students With Severe Disabilities
  http://ceedar.education.ufl.edu/wp-content/uploads/2014/09/IC-3_FINAL_03-03-15.pdf
- National Autism Association
  http://nationalautismassociation.org
- National Autism Center
  http://www.nationalautismcenter.org
- National Professional Development Center for ASD
  http://autismpdc.fpg.unc.edu
- Ohio Center for Low Incidence Disabilities
  http://www.ocali.org

Recommended Reading

Alberto, P., & Troutman, A. (2012). *Applied behavior analysis for teachers* (9th ed.). Upper Saddle River, NJ: Prentice Hall.

Collins, B. C. (2012). *Systematic instruction for students with moderate and severe disabilities.* Baltimore, MD: Paul H. Brookes Publishing Co.

REFLECTION QUESTIONS

1. The NPDC (http://autismpdc.fpg.unc.edu) and the NAC (http://www.nationalautism center.org/national-standards-project) have identified evidence-based practices or treatments for students with ASD. Compare and contrast the two reports. Be sure to identify the differences in identified practices, categories of practices, and measurement criteria used by each group to categorize practices.

2. Many myths surround treatments, therapies, and instructional methods for students with ASD. Choose an evidence-based practice not listed in Table 3.1. Research that practice in the report from the NPDC or the NAC to determine why it was not included as an evidence-based practice. Follow up by finding one peer-reviewed article studying that practice. Discuss how educators should approach such practices. When is it okay to use them, and when should they never be used? How can a school leader know?

3. The CEC has established professional ethical principles and practice standards (https://www.cec.sped.org/Standards/Ethical-Principles-and-Practice-Standards). How can an educational leader facilitate the implementation of this standard in programs, in practices, and with service providers of students with ASD?

4 The Evidence-Based Classroom Observation Tool for Creating Building- and District-Level Capacity

Christina R. Carnahan, K. Alisa Lowrey, and Kate Snyder

QUESTIONS THIS CHAPTER WILL ANSWER

1. What are the three categories of the EBP COT?
2. What are the subsections under each category?
3. What are the indicators in each category or subsection?
4. How is each indicator scored? Describe an example for each.
5. What process is involved in scoring each section of the EBP COT?

The EBP COT was developed after a request from administrators who were unclear about the supports and strategies responsive to the needs of students with ASD. Similarly, many teachers indicated they were looking for a way to "be on the same page" with school leaders visiting their classrooms and promote high levels of engagement and learning for their students. The perspectives of these stakeholders highlighted the need for clarity and common language in developing learning environments for students with ASD. This spirit of communication and collaboration ultimately led to the development of the EBP COT—a simple checklist to support teachers, school leaders, families, and other professionals when planning and assessing learning environments for students with ASD. The purpose of the EBP COT is to support school teams in collaboratively designing and implementing high-quality instruction for students with ASD. The EBP COT allows for briefly observing and benchmarking the components of a highly effective learning environment.

The EPB COT contains three broad categories—environmental, instructional, and communication considerations (see Figure 4.1). Each category incorporates best practices for students with ASD identified by leading professional organizations (e.g., NPDC, CEC's competencies for teachers of students with ASD, and the NAC). Appendix Table 1 contains a crosswalk between the EBPs identified by the National Professional Development Center on ASD and the National Autism Center and the corresponding sections of the EBP COT. The crosswalk is intended to highlight connections between the EBP COT and specific EBPs. It is *not* meant as an exhaustive list, nor is the intent to provide specific examples. Rather, when teams identify gaps illustrated through the COT, they should be able to map back to the EBP for additional support and training.

This chapter is broken in three separate sections, one for each category on the EBP COT. Each section describes the indicators necessary for creating effective programming for students with ASD and details the guidelines for scoring. Specifically, the sections contain a description of the category indicators and a scoring guide for each of the indicators.

GENERAL SCORING STRUCTURE

The EBP COT is scored on a 4-point scale from 0 to 3. Although the tool can be used in many ways, this chapter specifically focuses on scoring during an observation, including specific examples of evidence (see Figures 4.2–4.7). The following steps will help guide educators' observations and ensure follow-up:

1. Make sure all team members review the EBP COT before the observation.

2. Spend 10 minutes observing the instructional setting and consider observing additional environments as appropriate (e.g., art, music, physical education, the playground, the lunchroom).

3. Plan a follow-up meeting soon after the observation.
   - Ask clarifying questions and discuss strengths and opportunities for growth during the follow-up meeting.
   - Prioritize next steps for implementing the prioritized indicators.
     i. Identify any needed resources.
     ii. Create a timeline and plan for implementation.

The EBP COT is not intended for evaluating educators or other professionals, and scores from observations say nothing about a teacher's skill or value. These scores are intended to help teams prioritize steps to ensure increasingly valuable learning environments for students with ASD. The goal of the EBP COT is to help teams identify areas of strength and prioritize opportunities for growth in the educational settings observed, with a focus toward improving the educational success of students with ASD.

Universal Design for Learning (UDL; CAST, 2011) is the theoretical foundation on which the EBP COT is nested and is beneficial for general educators to use when designing inclusive classrooms. UDL is a framework for curriculum design that includes attention to environmental design, instructional methods, materials, goals, and assessments, with the ultimate goal of supporting all learners. Teachers report successful use of implementation in general education classes that include students with ASD and other developmental

Date/time: _____   Teacher: _____   Observer: _____

Number of students/grade: _____   Number of staff in classroom: _____   Instructional activity/content: _____

ENVIRONMENTAL

PHYSICAL ORGANIZATION

1. Classroom spaces are defined by visual and physical arrangement (e.g., furniture arrangement)

2. Classroom areas include identifiable spaces for various instructional configurations (check ✓ any of the following observed)
   - Independent work
   - Large group
   - Small group
   - One-to-one instruction
   - Other (please describe):

3. Instructionally relevant classroom materials are visible and well organized

VISUAL SCHEDULES

4a. Overall classroom schedule is posted and easy to read (where every student and every staff member should be at any given time)

4b. Students receive instruction (in academic, functional, or social-communication skills) that corresponds to the schedule(s)

5a. Staff schedules posted (may be embedded in master classroom schedule)

5b. Adults are in assigned areas as indicated on the schedule, or teachers can articulate valid reason for change

6a. Every student has an individualized schedule (e.g., object, picture based, text based) that he or she can manipulate

6b. Students' schedules are designed for use across activities and environments

6c. Systematic instruction is used to teach students to independently use their schedules

BEHAVIORAL SUPPORTS

7. Visual supports communicate classroom rules and expectations (e.g., text based, pictures)

8. Reinforcement used across classroom activities

9. Staff offers choices

10. Staff honors student choices as earned or requested

11. Transitions between tasks and activities occur quickly and with minimal disruptions

12. Individualized transition supports (e.g., wait chairs, transition area) are available for students as they move between activities or environments

INSTRUCTIONAL CONSIDERATIONS

13. Indicate the type(s) of instruction observed in the classroom during the observation
    - Independent work
    - Whole group
    - Small group
    - Individualized instruction with adult or peer
    - Other (please describe):

14. Goals of instructional activities are clearly identifiable to observer without explanation

15. Activity schedules or work systems are used to communicate expectations including the activity to complete, amount required, and what will occur upon completion during all instructional activities

16. Individualized work systems are used for independent work tasks to communicate activity to complete, how to complete, amount required, and what will occur upon completion

17. Additional environmental supports are embedded in classroom instruction (check ✓ any of the following that were observed during instructional activities; mark any of the following that were observed in the classroom, but not used in instructional activities, with an "x")
    - Visual timers
    - Token economy
    - First/then instructions
    - Graphic organizers
    - Templates
    - Visual directions
    - Choice template (e.g., written list, picture icons)
    - Video models
    - Other (please describe):

18. Systematic instruction includes gaining attention, direction (prompting), student response, and feedback—either error correction or reinforcement

19. Classroom activities include direct instruction in building independence
    - Meaningful skill and independence
    - Academic independence

20. Staff actively participate with students in learning or in classroom-related activities (e.g., preparing materials)

21. Staff are observed collecting data on student performance

22. Conversation among staff limited to discussion directly related to curriculum, instruction, and classroom activities

COMMUNICATION

23. Communication systems (e.g., assistive technology) are utilized in the classroom to support students with communication differences

24. Staff members do not speak on behalf of students and instead encourage and/or prompt students to use expressive communication

25. Communication instruction is embedded throughout classroom activities

26. Direct instruction in social interaction is embedded throughout classroom activities

27. All students have opportunities to communicate with both peers and adults
    - Adults
    - Peers

Scoring Guide

0 = N/A
1 = No or very limited implementation
2 = Partial implementation
3 = Full implementation

*Please review scoring guide for clarity in numerical values, specific examples in each category, and references, citations, and resources.

Figure 4.1. Evidence-Based Practices Classroom Observation Tool.

Facilitating Evidence-Based Practice for Students with ASD: A Classroom Observation Tool for Building Quality Education by Christina R. Carnahan and K. Alisa Lowrey.
Copyright © 2018 by Paul H. Brookes Publishing Co., Inc. All rights reserved.

disabilities (Dymond et al., 2006; Lowrey, Hollingshead, Howery, & Bishop, 2017). UDL includes 31 checkpoints that guide teachers to anticipate learner variability in the classroom and plan multiple means to address that variability through ways content is represented, ways students are active and engaged, and ways students share what they know (CAST, 2015). UDL is included in the ESSA and is one way to bridge those individualized needs of learners with disabilities into the curricular design and planning of general educators. UDL may serve as a framework that helps administrators impress the importance of designing educational experiences using a collaborative planning model on general and special educators (see Chapter 5). Many of the considerations discussed next can be addressed through the UDL framework.

ENVIRONMENTAL CONSIDERATIONS

"Simply stated, unless there is a foundation of structure that underpins each learner's educational program, even the most robust and potentially effective method will be relatively useless and inept" (Simpson, Mundschenk, & Heflin, 2011, p. 13). These words highlight the critical nature of a well-organized environment and underscore the importance of environmental considerations for all learners with ASD. Environmental considerations are essential for optimizing learning for students with ASD and, thus, compose the first category in the EBP COT. Educators minimize the organizational, memory, and attention challenges learners with ASD face every day by implementing the environmental structures and supports outlined in this section of the tool. Furthermore, learners are better able to focus on academics, social-communication, and behavioral targets that prepare them for success at home, in their communities, and in their lives after high school when these challenges are minimized.

The environmental considerations category focuses on strategies that support a well-structured learning environment including overall organization, scheduling, providing choice, embedding behavioral supports, defining physical areas, and facilitating transitions (Iovannone et al., 2003). The environmental considerations category focuses on three specific areas—physical organization, visual schedules, and behavioral supports.

Physical Organization

Physical organization is not only the foundation for creating an optimal learning setting for students with ASD, but well-organized physical spaces also serve as the framework on which other critical supports and instructional strategies for students with ASD are built. Physical organization includes three specific indicators—visually well-defined spaces, varied instructional configurations, and material organization.

Use Visuals to Define Space (Indicator 1) Using physical structures to visually define space within the instructional environment is one important way educators support students with ASD (Hume, 2008; Iovanne et al., 2003). Educators visually define learning spaces when they employ furniture arrangements to communicate boundaries within the classroom and use labels to illustrate the purpose of each instructional area (Mesibov & Shea, 2010). For example, a science teacher who implements a well-defined physical space uses physical boundaries to communicate the activities and expectations within a lesson (e.g., rows of desks for lectures, tables for small-group work). Similarly, a librarian who uses bookshelves to create spaces for read-alouds that are clearly separated from individual chairs for silent reading is also applying the principles of physical structures to create well-defined physical spaces. The teacher and librarian are doing more than just communicating behavioral expectations; they are helping students know where to direct their attention.

Many educators remark that they do not have enough space in their classrooms to create such well-structured, organized physical environments. These educators often cite reasons small spaces are challenging, such as difficulty designating areas for specific tasks or being unable to include all the activities or materials needed within one classroom. Small spaces can pose challenges, but smaller spaces are often easier to organize than large, wide open classrooms. Providing clear information about what will happen in a space at a certain time and maintaining a high level of organization are ultimately the keys to success.

Include Options for Various Instructional Configurations (Indicator 2) Indicator 2 addresses the instructional configuration or groupings. Students with ASD benefit from a variety of instructional strategies and interventions that occur in one-to-one, independent, small-group, and large-group settings. One-to-one discrete trial training (Fleury, 2013), peer-mediated instruction in pairs or small groups (Neitzel, 2008), or individual or group social skills instruction (Fettig, 2013) are examples of evidence-based practices that require varied instructional groups. Thus, well-organized instructional spaces should include options for various instructional configurations to meet the needs of students with ASD.

Educators face a variety of challenges when implementing multiple instructional configurations for learners with ASD. For example, many students with ASD may have difficulty understanding the different behavioral expectations that correspond with each of the instructional configurations. Large-group lessons often involve sitting quietly on the floor or at desks, facing a teacher and shifting between what the teacher is saying and other instructional materials. Yet, learners are often expected to work with materials in an organized, self-directed manner during independent activities, often problem solving how to move from one step or activity to another. Visually defined spaces can help communicate behavioral expectations for various activities in the schedule, but it is essential to systematically teach students with ASD how to participate in each type of instructional activity. In addition, strategies such as video models, picture or written schedules or directions, and rehearsals can also support students in engaging in different classroom activities.

Many teachers face challenges across grade levels when students struggle to work independently or participate in small or large groups. The following four points should be considered:

1. *What are the current structures and supports in place?* After identifying the existing structures, consider challenging the team to creatively add more structures.

2. *How could the flexibility of the materials and the content be increased?* This question encourages the team to think flexibly about the kinds of materials used to represent the content. For example, music, videos, or even concrete objects could be used to represent the concepts, rather than spoken or printed words. This question also helps educators think about how the student responds to the material. For example, the student selects from or matches a set of pictures (or even just one to start) to respond to the concepts, rather than responding verbally or in writing.

3. *What skills should be taught so the student is able to participate?* Focus on what needs to be taught to increase success, rather than on why the student cannot

participate in groups or work independently. Shifting the focus helps create an actionable plan to increase the learner's engagement and independence. These steps can be small and include skills such as sitting in a chair and facing a teacher, but they can also be more complex such as responding to questions from a peer or asking an on-topic question.

4. *How can flexibility be increased?* Students with ASD may struggle with various instructional considerations because of difficulty regulating their bodies or they have not developed the ability to attend for an extended amount of time. This does not mean the student cannot learn the content. Nor does it mean the learner, even students in late adolescence, will never be able to participate in the group or activity. Flexible participation may be a critical first step toward gaining access to the content and setting. Walking in the back of the classroom, sitting on a ball, or simply standing to complete their work are options for increasing flexibility for these students. A more comprehensive approach might be helpful for other students. For example, a student could watch a brief video model, make the transition to the group or assigned work task, and sit for just a minute or two, receiving frequent reinforcement. The student could then make the transition away from the group or task to a one-to-one setting to work with materials related to the instructional topic and then take a brief break. This process could be repeated several times in a 20-minute lesson.

Organize Learning Materials (Indicator 3) Chapter 1 described the EF differences that are characteristic of many students with ASD. The impact of these differences on response inhibition and flexibility can be significant. Pay close attention to instructional materials to mitigate the possible challenges these differences may cause in the classroom. Extraneous materials can create a distraction for all students but particularly for students with ASD who often demonstrate greater difficulty regulating their own attention (Attwood, 2008). Only materials with a clearly identifiable instructional purpose should be accessible during instruction to better support the overall organization of the classroom.

In addition to limiting instructional materials to only those necessary, creating highly structured materials is a critical aspect of organized learning materials (Mesibov & Schopler, 2010). Mesibov and Schopler provided the guidelines for task organization. Specific or individual tasks should be organized to indicate exactly what the learner will do and how he or she will do it and provide clear indicators of completion. The overarching, or perhaps even simple idea, is that the expectations of every task, including where to start, what to do, and when or how to finish, should be clear. Structured tasks are valuable for individuals across grade levels and in a variety of settings. For example, highly structured tasks can be used to support participation in art activities for young children or employment for young adults.

Scoring Physical Organization Specific examples and scoring guidelines for the indicators in the physical organization section of the EBP COT are detailed in Figure 4.2. The indicators for visual definitions, instructional configurations, and relevant instructional materials are typically scorable even in circumstances when direct instruction is not occurring. The following three indicators should be clear when observing the physical environment:

1. *Classroom space visually defined.* This indicator can be viewed from the "stranger test" perspective. If a visitor is unable to determine the purpose of an area of the classroom, then it is very likely a student with ASD might also be unsure. Similarly,

Physical Organization		
Item	Examples	Scoring guidelines
1. Classroom spaces are defined by visual and physical arrangement (e.g., furniture arrangement such as using rugs, tape, or labels to define spaces for specific activities)	Desks for individual work are arranged in rows; a table and chairs at the back of the room are labeled "group work" The "literacy corner" is labeled and separated from the area labeled "math workshop" using a rug and bookcases A kidney-shaped table in the classroom is affixed with Velcro in which various signs are placed indicating which of the table's multiple purposes is in practice (e.g., group work, snack)	1 = physical space appears disorganized or difficult for students to independently maneuver 2 = physical space is organized but lacks clarity in the purpose of each space 3 = physical classroom space is well organized and visually defined; the purpose of each space is clear
2. Classroom areas include identifiable spaces for various instructional configurations (check any of the following observed) Independent work ☐ Large group ☐ Small group ☐ One-to-one instruction ☐ Other:_____ ☐	Small groups of three to four desks are arranged in a manner that centralizes the white board/SMART board (e.g., independent, small group, large group) A small table beside the teacher's desk is labeled "work with teacher" (one-to-one instruction) Desks for individual work are arranged in rows A table and chairs at the back of the room are labeled "group work"	1 = classroom design appears to accommodate one instructional configuration 2 = classroom design appears to accommodate two configurations 3 = classroom design appears to accommodate three or more configurations
3. Instructionally relevant classroom materials are visible and well organized (i.e., nonrelevant or distracting materials are minimized)	Open shelving in the classroom contains age-appropriate reading materials and containers with labels such as "science journals" or "math practice activities" Nonexample: Staff members' personal belongings in instructional space Stacks of papers, books, and so forth covering instructional areas	1 = instructional setting contains the necessary materials, but the setting is disorganized/cluttered, or the materials are not prepared and available 2 = instructional setting contains the materials necessary for the lesson; other materials are also present but setting lacks clarity as to which materials are for the lesson and which are not 3 = instructional setting only contains materials relevant to instruction, or the instructor organizes the instructional setting in a way that makes it clear which materials the students will use and how they apply to the lesson

Figure 4.2. Environmental considerations: Physical organization.

a visitor might easily note a variety of things in the environment that seem unrelated to instruction (e.g., piles of paper and other materials on group tables, open boxes of various materials stacked on shelves).

2. *Varied instructional configurations (e.g., independent, small group, one to one).* The instructional configurations indicator is scored slightly different from other sections.

- Use a checkmark or tally mark to indicate each configuration observed (e.g., one to one, independent, group).

- If only one instructional configuration is observed (e.g., a single rows of desks), then provide a score of "0" (not observed) because multiple configurations were not apparent.

3. *Only instructionally relevant classroom materials are visible and well organized.* This indicator highlights the importance of providing access to materials that are instructionally relevant and organizing the materials in a way that communicates exactly what the student should do and how he or she should do it.

The instructional configurations indicator highlights why the EBP COT is not intended to be evaluative, but it is to be used as a catalyst for collaboration and conversation. Discussion with the classroom teacher might indicate desk organization is constrained by furniture availability or classroom layout. The teacher may adjust the rows of desks to allow for partner work or even small groups, but those configurations may not be observed during a classroom visit.

Visual Schedules

Visual schedules are a critical evidence-based practice for meeting the instructional needs of students with ASD (e.g., Bryan & Gast, 2000; Cihak, 2011; Morrison, Sainato, Benchaaban, & Endo, 2002; O'Reilly, Sigafoos, Lancioni, Edrisinha, & Andrews, 2005). These schedules can include the overall classroom schedule and schedules for individual students (Mesibov et al., 2005; Scheuermann & Webber, 2002). A well-structured learning environment includes both types of schedules to clarify roles and activities, facilitate transitions, and ensure that all participants in the instructional environment (educators included) are operating from the same set of temporal and sequential expectations across the school day.

Classroom Schedules (Indicators 4 and 5) Indicators 4 and 5 address the overall classroom schedules and the associated staff schedules and behaviors. Classroom schedules communicate the overall class activities, are fairly consistent over time (e.g., across a semester or term), and clarify the "who," "what," "where," and "when" of the classroom (i.e., what students are doing at any given time throughout the school day and where it is occurring). Overall schedules should be 1) visible and easily read from anywhere in the instructional environment and 2) include information about the educator's schedule either embedded in the overall schedule or posted separately (Meadan, Ostrosky, Triplett, Michna, & Fettig, 2011). The goals of a classroom schedule are to ensure that all adult team members know where to be at all times, and, theoretically, another adult could step into the role of the educator if necessary without loss of significant instructional time.

Scoring Overall Schedules (Indicators 4 and 5) **(Figure 4.3)** Look for the following items when scoring the overall schedule section:

- An overall classroom schedule posted somewhere in the classroom
- Information about where the adults in the classroom are teaching or working
- The extent to which the classroom activities match those posted on the schedule

In addition to noting the presence of schedules during an observation, also note whether students and educators engage in activities that correspond to the posted schedule. If there is not a match, then consider talking with the team about discrepancies. If they can articulate a reason for the difference in either a student or adult schedule, then the score should be "0" (not applicable).

Student Schedules (Indicators 6 and 7) Indicators 6 and 7 address individual student schedules, application across environments, and systematic instruction to support students in using their schedules. Individual schedules communicate expectations and

Visual Schedules		
Item	Examples	Scoring guidelines
4a. Overall classroom schedule is posted and easy to read (where every student and every staff member should be at any given time)	A classroom schedule is printed on poster-size paper and posted on the wall A lesson schedule is legibly printed on the white board in an 11th-grade chemistry classroom	1 = schedule is available but not posted, or there is no schedule available 2 = an overall schedule is posted, but it is not large enough to read from a distance 3 = clear schedule is posted and is easy to read
4b. Students receive instruction (in academic, functional, or social-communication skills) that corresponds to the schedule(s)	The schedule indicates center time, and all students are participating in a classroom-based center The schedule on the board indicates the order of classroom activities in the biology lab: 1) independent review sheet, 2) group lesson, 3) work with partner, 4) complete and submit lab assignment All students are working with a partner in the lab according to the schedule	0 (N/A) = the educator can articulate a valid reason for a change (e.g., a student is in his or her "home base" area to calm down following a stressful event) 1 = little or no instruction 2 = instruction is occurring but does not correspond to schedule or if a necessary change in the schedule (e.g., an absent related services provider) was not communicated to students 3 = instruction is occurring and corresponds to what is on the schedule
5a. Staff schedules posted (may be embedded in master classroom schedule)	The overall schedule hanging on the wall includes a staff member's name beside each activity or location A separate staff schedule is posted on the wall indicating the activity, group, or location for which each staff is responsible throughout the day	0 (N/A) = the educator is the only staff member in the room 1 = staff schedules are available but not posted, or staff schedules are not available 2 = staff schedules are available and are posted for parts of the day 3 = staff schedules are posted, and it is clear where all adults should be throughout the day
5b. Adults are in assigned areas as indicated in the schedule, or teacher can articulate valid reason for change	The schedule indicates that Mr. X is working with a small group for math, Ms. C. is supervising independent work and leisure time, Mrs. H. is working one to one with a student, and all three are in the indicated locations Mr. X and Ms. C. are in the locations indicated by the schedule, but Mr. X indicates that Mrs. H. is outside of the classroom with a student who requested a walk as a calming strategy	1 = no schedule is posted, and educator assignments cannot be confirmed, or educators are not in assigned areas 2 = most educators are in assigned areas, or there is a change, but staff cannot articulate reasons for change 3 = all educators are in assigned areas, or the staff are able to articulate clear reasons for the change

Figure 4.3. Scoring overall visual schedules.

a sequence of events across the school day (Mesibov et al., 2005). Ensure individual schedules are designed to meet each student's unique needs (Knight, Sartini, & Spriggs, 2015) because their ultimate goal is to promote independence, engagement, and learning (Mesibov, Browder, & Kirkland, 2002). For example, a student who does not read text needs a picture-based schedule, a student who reads some text may have a schedule that incorporates pictures and words, and another student may have a completely written schedule.

Designing schedules for use across activities and environments throughout the school day is another important consideration (Hume, 2008). For example, if a student has a written, check-off schedule posted on a desk in one of the classrooms, then it is important to consider how the student will apply the schedule to activities that occur in direct succession outside of the classroom (e.g., physical education followed by lunch, followed by recess).

Developing and implementing individual schedules is an essential programming component for learners with ASD (Hume, 2008). Several resources exist to support educators in the process, and two are included at the end of this chapter. The following section offers a few considerations to support teams in changing the complexity and sophistication of individual schedules to meet each student's needs and support problem solving when students struggle with implementation. Supporting students to use visual schedules involves systematically teaching each learner how to use the schedule. Systematic teaching is not addressed in this portion of the text or checklist, but the specific considerations described later are important to the success of visual schedules.

A few common ways to individualize the complexity of a schedule include altering the presentation format, the visual symbols, and the amount of information contained in the schedule (Banda, Grimmett, & Hart, 2009). First, consider the presentation format. Schedules can be effectively presented in many ways (Knight et al., 2015), including written checklists, videos, and symbols (e.g., pictures, written words, objects) students carry with them from one location to the next. In addition, consider the amount of information contained within an individual schedule. Some students can manage a list of activities that will occur across the entire school day, whereas others benefit from seeing only two activities at a time. Each learner's strengths, needs, and interests should ultimately guide decisions about the how to present the schedule and the amount of information included.

Selecting the visual symbol format that aligns with the student's understanding is a second consideration. Some learners benefit from concrete representation (e.g., photographs, objects), whereas others do well with more abstract symbols (e.g., colored line drawings, printed words) (Banda et al., 2009; Scheuermann & Webber, 2002). Thus, if a student struggles to follow his or her schedule, then consider how well the individual understands the symbols used to communicate each activity as well as the presentation mode and number of activities or tasks included. Similarly, once the student independently uses his or her schedule, consider strategies for building the complexity by incorporating more sophisticated presentation formats, increasing abstract symbols, and increasing the number of tasks the schedule communicates.

Scoring Individual Schedules (Indicators 6 and 7)   Some individuals with ASD are successful when they follow the classwide, overall schedule. In such cases, Item 7a ("Every student has an individualized visual schedule . . .") should be scored "0" (not applicable). Yet, most students with ASD not only benefit from but also need individual schedules to be successful and independent, even if the schedule is in the form of an electronic list in their cell phone. Thus, look for the following when scoring this section of the checklist:

- *The presence and use of individualized schedules for all students with ASD.* Each student in the class should have a schedule individualized to meet his or her needs and that he or she can use independently.

- *Schedules that can be used in environments throughout the school.* Schedules should be created for students to use across environments whenever possible. If a schedule appears to be applicable for only one environment, then discuss with the teacher how schedules are implemented in other environments.

- *Systematic instruction, as appropriate, to teach students to use their individual schedules.* Consider whether students are using schedules without support. If so, enter a score of "0" (not applicable). If not, educators should be using systematic prompting strategies (e.g., gestural prompts) to teach students to use the schedules. If educators are directing students to the next activity using verbal directions or without encouraging the use of the schedule, then score the item as "1" (not observed).

Figure 4.4 provides a detailed description of the considerations for scoring the items related to individual visual schedules. Visual schedules are perhaps the most important of the environmental structures because they support independent participation across

Visual Schedules		
Item	Examples	Scoring guidelines
6a. Every student has an individualized schedule (e.g., object, picture based, text based) that he or she can manipulate (i.e., physically access) independently	One student is using a schedule with picture icons affixed with Velcro that are matched to the corresponding picture in instructional areas, whereas another student uses a laminated written schedule with a check box for completion column that is taped to his or her desk A student has a schedule application on his or her iPad or a written schedule in a notebook that is used between classes Nonexample: Every student in the classroom has the same picture icon schedule despite individual student differences (e.g., inability to independently physically manipulate an icon that size, inability to distinguish between picture icons)	0 (N/A) = all students are observed independently using classwide schedule 1 = schedules are not available, or schedules are available but do not match the individual understanding level of each student (e.g., a student who does not read is presented with a written schedule) 2 = some students have access to a schedule, and the schedule matches their understanding (e.g., a reader uses a written schedule, a nonreader uses appropriate pictures) 3 = each student has access to a visual schedule he or she can manipulate independently, and the schedule clearly matches the learner's understanding (i.e., the schedule is neither too sophisticated or challenging nor not complex enough)
6b. Students' schedules are designed for use across activities and environments	A student has his or her daily schedule embedded within his or her planner and carries it from class to class A student's two-step (first/then) schedule is made with miniobjects affixed with Velcro to the outside of a binder that can be carried throughout the school building	1 = no schedules are present, or schedules are present, but students do not use the schedules 2 = schedules are available and used in some environments but not all, or schedules are available and used across the day, but they are not individualized to specific students 3 = all students have schedules that support them in moving throughout their day and in various environments as appropriate
6c. Systematic instruction is used to teach students to independently use their schedules	A classroom paraprofessional uses gestural prompting strategies to teach independent schedule use (e.g., points to the location of the schedule on the wall) A student is handed a card with the words *check schedule* written on it after finishing a classroom activity Nonexample: Adults tell students where they will be going next without systematically prompting independent schedule use. For example, an educator says, "John, you have physical education next" without directing John to check his schedule, or the teacher takes an icon off a student's schedule without prompting the student to do so independently.	0 (N/A) = students use their schedules independently 1 = schedules are available, and students do not use the schedules; students clearly do not know how to use the schedules and no teaching procedures are in place; or no schedules are available 2 = students are observed using schedules incorrectly without systematic teaching to correct the error 3 = clear teaching processes are in place to support students in using their schedules throughout the day, or all students are independently using schedules

Figure 4.4. Scoring considerations for individual visual schedules.

settings, academic engagement, and positive behavior. The behavioral supports described in the next section are imperative, but visual schedules provide the foundation for their success when used in the context of well-structured learning environments.

Behavioral Supports

Behavioral supports represent the third category under environmental consideration in the EBP COT. The four behavioral support indicators highlighted in the EBP COT include visual supports, reinforcement, choice, and structured transitions. These four approaches are proactive strategies designed to help students understand and meet expectations throughout the school day. The ultimate goal is to ensure engagement, learning, and increasing levels of independence.

Visual Supports Used to Communicate Classroom Rules and Expectations (Indicator 7)
In addition to visual schedules, other visual supports are critical for promoting positive behavior and helping students with ASD function independently across learning environments (Kellems, Gabrielsen, & Williams, 2016; Mavropoulou, Papadopoulou, & Kakana, 2011). These visuals come in many forms and serve many purposes, but the ultimate goal is to translate information otherwise provided verbally, or perhaps even inferred from the environment, into a concrete format for students (Sam & AFIRM, 2015). Students with ASD benefit from visuals used to 1) communicate rules, expectations, and directions (Carnahan & Snyder, 2011); 2) increase independent transitions within and between activities (Hume, Sreckovic, Snyder, & Carnahan, 2014); 3) organize academic tasks (e.g., graphic organizers) (Knight et al., 2015); and 4) promote behavior regulation (e.g., self-management) (Carr, Moore, & Anderson, 2014). The format of a visual support often includes pictures, printed words, videos, simple color-coding, or a combination (Hume et al., 2014). Examples of visual supports include picture or written class rules posted in the front of the classroom and provided to the individual with ASD, color-coding to indicate the specific behavioral or activity expectations, and providing structured graphic organizers during academic instruction to help students direct their attention. The types of visual support beneficial to an individual may change depending on age or setting. The goal for many individuals is not to get rid of the supports but to independently request and manage increasingly sophisticated supports.

One simple example of visual supports comes from a high school science teacher who used construction paper taped to his classroom door to indicate whether the lesson would be a lecture (indicated by a piece of blue construction paper) or lab (indicated by a piece of red paper). After teaching the specific rules of each lesson format, the teacher provided students with color-coded written rules to keep in their binders. This structure set the stage for participation and learning for all students before they entered the classroom. The teacher provided students with a structured document for taking notes during lectures.

Guided notes that align with or follow the same structure and format of a lecture not only direct students' attention to the salient points but also help organize their thinking about a concept. Figure 4.5 provides an example of a highly structured format for note taking. Although this document can be adapted to fit a variety of topics, it is currently structured to support a lecture in which a teacher is describing a concept. The form should be modified to align with the specific purpose and structure of a lecture.

In summary, visual supports promote independence, learning, and self-management for students with ASD. They can be used in academic and social settings to communicate expectations, promote independence and self-regulation, and help individuals organize information. Increasing an individuals' ability to use visual supports could ultimately support their success in personal, educational, and employment settings, thereby improving their overall quality of life.

Reinforcement (Indicator 8) Reinforcement creates a relationship between a behavior or skill and a corresponding consequence (Neitzel, 2008) and should be embedded within instructional activities to promote learning and positive behavior for students with ASD. Implementing reinforcement systems in schools can be complex (Kelly & Barnes-Homes, 2015; Maag, 2001) and at times controversial. Advances in schoolwide positive behavior interventions and supports (PBIS), however, has placed an increasing focus on proactive strategies (Horner & Sugai, 2015). One example of PBIS in schools is when educators systematically teach students specific desired behavior and continually look for students demonstrating the behaviors, providing reinforcement in the form of behavior-specific praise

Topic	
Big idea (what we will learn)	
Essential detail one	My notes:	Brief summary or question:
Essential detail two	My notes:	Brief summary or question:
Essential detail three	My notes:	Brief summary or question:
Summary	

Figure 4.5. Structured notetaking format.

or even a tangible item (Shuster et al., 2017). These strategies not only decrease behavioral incidents but can also promote positive school climates (Bradshaw, Koth, Thornton, & Leaf, 2009).

Many of the strategies utilized in schoolwide PBIS are rooted in the concepts of ABA (Horner & Sugai, 2015), which is also the theoretical foundation in which reinforcement is rooted. Systematically teaching desired behavior and providing reinforcement promotes skill development for students with ASD. In fact, systematic reinforcement often leads to decreases in challenging behavior (Martinez, Werch, & Conroy, 2016), increased skill acquisition (Karsten & Carr, 2009), and even self-control (Dixon & Cummins, 2001). More important, students with ASD can be taught to delay reinforcement and self-monitor their own behavior when systematic systems are implemented (Whiting & Dixon, 2015). Understanding a few key concepts increases the likelihood that reinforcement systems will be effective.

- *Understand reinforcement.* A consequence must increase the likelihood of the behavior or skill occurring over time to be considered reinforcing. Reinforcement can be positive (the delivery of something after a desired response or behavior) or negative (the removal of a nonpreferred object or activity after a desired response or behavior). For example, using a predetermined effective reinforce for a student, a teacher may allow the student to earn the reinforcement by completing an assigned task. For example, a student may complete an identified number of math problems during independent work time to play a preferred math game immediately following. The math game works as a reinforcer if access to it increases the number of math problems the student completes during independent work time.

- *Identify the behavior to increase.* Members of the team need to be able to recognize the behavior in order to reinforce it. Clearly defining and sharing a description helps ensure all team members will be able to recognize the behavior when it occurs.

- *Determine student preferences.* Determining student preferences sets the foundation for selecting reinforcement. Identifying a list of several items, activities, or people can help ensure a student does not become bored or uninterested. In addition, a list of several items allows teams to create a match between the effort required for the student to do the desired behavior and the reinforcement (Karsten, Carr, & Lepper, 2011).

- *Individualize reinforcement.* What works for one learner will not necessarily work for others. Understanding a student's preferences not only helps align the intensity of the reinforcement with the response effort required but can also drive individualization of reinforcement systems. The schedule with which reinforcement is delivered is another point for individualization. Individual reinforcement schedules can be modified as students develop and increase independence with specific desired behaviors.

Offering and Honoring Choice (Indicators 9 and 10) Indicators 9 and 10 address choices for students with ASD. Offering choice (Indicator 9) is a critical antecedent-based intervention for students with ASD (Neitzel, 2008; Reutebuch, El Zein, & Roberts, 2015). Choice making not only promotes positive behavior but is also the foundation for self-determination (Wehmeyer & Shogren, 2016). In addition to offering choices, it is important for educators to honor the choices students make. Beukelman and Mirenda (2013) described choice making as the process that occurs "when an individual selects a preferred item or activity from two or more options, either independently or when someone else offers them" (2005, p. 292). It is important to remember that choice making is not the same as requesting, and although individuals often communicate with others about their choices, choice making does not necessarily occur within a communication event. Thus, although choice making is not a communicative act at its core, it is the foundation for making decisions and a critical first step in communicating with others about those decisions.

Educators increase engagement, attention, and learning for all students when they offer choices (Royer, Lane, Cantwell, & Messenger, 2017). Educators can offer choices to students throughout the day, often without interrupting the flow of instruction. Providing students with options within a lesson (e.g., reading silently or listening to an audiobook; offering options for dictating, handwriting, or typing a writing assignment), allowing students to select something to do after a lesson (e.g., spending time on the computer, reading a book, coloring), or allowing freedom to select a topic to study are ways in which educators can seamlessly build in choices. Teachers may naturally encourage engagement for all learners, including students with ASD, by building choices into the school day.

Some students, especially those with complex communication needs, may need systematic instruction to learn to make independent choices. Beukelman and Mirenda (2005) and Sigafoos, O'Reilly, and Lancioni (2009) provided detailed discussions regarding the process of and strategies for supporting choice making for students with ASD. A few points can help guide initial problem solving. First, consider if and how the student demonstrates preferences. Students may initially need to make basic selections between a preferred and nonpreferred item or two preferred items. Second, consider whether the student has a system for demonstrating his or her choices. Communication systems are specifically addressed later in this chapter, but if a student does not have a mode or way to demonstrate choice, then choice making will be limited. Next, consider whether the student has sufficient opportunities to make choices throughout the school day. As with all skills, the more opportunities to practice, the faster the skill will develop. Finally, consider whether the student is able to refuse or say no. Students need not only the ability to make choices but also to refuse or indicate when something is not a choice. Creating educational settings that encourage students to practice communication about preferences and nonpreferences will increase their ability to function independently across environments. It is important to see those opportunities for choice making when observing classrooms that include students with ASD.

Transition Supports (Indicators 11 and 12) Many students with ASD have difficulty making the transition between activities and environments (see Chapter 3) (Cihak, Fahrenkrog, Ayers, & Smith, 2010; Pierce, Spriggs, Gast, & Luscre, 2013). For the purpose of this text, transitions include moving from one environment to another or one activity to another, making the transition between different adults, or even moving from the carpet back to a desk within one classroom (Hall, Hollingshead, & Christman, 2017; Hume et al., 2014). Using supports is critical, regardless of the transition. Examples of valuable transition supports include timers indicating when one activity will end or another will begin, visual supports containing directions for a transition, and video models in which the steps in a transition are demonstrated.

Some students with ASD may need a specific location designated for transitions. These locations, often referred to as a *home base* (Coffin & Bassity, 2007), can include a desk or chair in a designated location, a locker, or even an office. When one activity is complete, the student returns to the designated location to check an individualized visual schedule and then make the transition to the next activity or location. Although this may seem time consuming, a transition area can increase the amount of time students spend academically engaged.

Hume and colleagues (2014) described a process for increasing the success of students with ASD as they transition throughout the day, including identifying times when transitions are challenging, selecting and implementing possible strategies, and ongoing data collection and problem solving. Although specific interventions or supports vary, the goal is to increase independence and engagement by preparing the student for transitions, providing clear guidelines or directions regarding expected behavior (i.e., what it looks like during the transition), increasing focus and attention, and providing additional information about the social context in which the transition occurs.

Increasing independence, building positive behavior, and promoting engagement should be the focus when implementing and teaching students to use specific transition-related supports (Hall et al., 2017; Iadarola et al., 2017). Thus, once transition supports are in place, ongoing analysis of the student's success is important (Hume et al., 2014). If the student continues to experience difficulty even with support in place, then the team should consider why the challenge persists. Possible considerations include insufficient systematic instruction, difficulty of the activities or tasks the student transitions between, environmental factors, or a mismatch between the selected intervention and needs of the learner. Conversely, if the student is more successful, then the team might consider strategies for increasing the sophistication, such as embedding the transition support on the student's cell phone, increasing the independence with which the student gains access to the support (e.g., teach the student to request the support rather than wait for teacher direction), or using the support at other times during the day both in and out of school.

Scoring Behavioral Supports

Figure 4.6 details the behavioral support indicators. Some behavioral indicators may be obvious when observing a classroom, whereas others may require a bit more attention to notice. Look for the following when observing for behavioral indicators:

Behavioral Supports		
Item	Examples	Scoring guidelines
7. Visual supports communicate classroom rules and expectations (e.g., text based, pictures)	A large poster in the classroom identifies the four classroom rules with a picture icon representing each rule Expectations for classroom routines, tasks, and procedures (e.g., handing in assignments, working in groups) are written and posted on the classroom walls	1 = no rules or expectations are posted, rules or expectations are posted but difficult to read, or there is little communication with students regarding these rules and expectations 2 = rules and expectations are posted and communicated to the group 3 = rules and expectations are posted and clearly communicated in a way that each student can understand; students who need individualized information about rules and expectations have the information available in a way they can understand
8. Reinforcement is used across classroom activities	Students are reinforced for displaying specified expectations (e.g., instructors provide immediate tangible reinforcement, such as stickers) following the completion of a task during one-to-one instruction with students A teacher gives frequent verbal praise to students in the classroom not only for correct responses but also for meeting behavioral expectations (e.g., remaining in seat during instruction, collaborating with peers during group work)	1 = no reinforcement is provided, some reinforcement is provided but not individualized to student preference, or some reinforcement is provided but the level does not match the task or behavioral demand 2 = reinforcement systems are in place but with little individualization, or reinforcement systems are in place but not communicated clearly to student 3 = clear systems for providing reinforcement, and systems are individualized for each student's needs
9. Staff offers choices	Students are given the option of choosing among a written report, a PowerPoint presentation, a video journal, or an online blog for a book report project Educator asks a student, "What would you like to work for today?" and offers a board with various picture icons of the student's preferred activities before beginning a task	1 = students have few or no choices during the day 2 = educators clearly plan for and offer choice during some activities during the day, or some choices may not account for individual student interests 3 = educators clearly plan for and offer choices throughout the day (i.e., during all academic, leisure/choice, and break times); choices are individualized to incorporate student interests
10. Staff honors student choices as earned or requested	Recognizing that only 5 minutes remain in the class period, the staff stop at a natural break in the lesson and give the students time for a preferred activity as promised at the beginning of class Nonexample: A student is not given the "swing time" he earned for completing independent work because the bell rang indicating the class was to make a transition to another room	1 = educator not observed offering choice 2 = some instructors honor students' choices, whereas others do not
11. Transitions between tasks and activities occur quickly and with minimal disruptions	A seventh-grade science teacher gives the entire class a 2-minute warning before a lab group rotation, then a verbal and gestural countdown from 5 seconds to indicate time to switch. To facilitate the rotation, the teacher says, "Rotate one station to the left. Check the chart on the board to be sure" and gestures to a chart indicating at which station each group would be during each rotation A timer goes off in the classroom at which point several students are given a card with a schedule picture icon, whereas others are given a verbal prompt to check their schedules	1 = transitions occur without warning, and expectations are not clear 2 = educators communicate when transitions will occur but provide limited information regarding expected behavior 3 = educators clearly communicate when transitions will occur

Figure 4.6. Scoring behavioral supports.

Behavioral Supports		
Item	Examples	Scoring guidelines
12. Individualized transition supports (e.g., home base or other transition area, visual timer) are available for students as they move between activities or environments	Educator hands a student a card that reads "wait chair," which directs the student to go to his or her desk between each rotation during a first-grade centers activity A sixth-grade student moves to his or her check-in area where he or she signs his or her name and checks his or her materials list when entering and leaving each classroom in his or her schedule	0 (N/A) = all students are observed independently making a transition between activities or environments 1 = no strategies for supporting students as they make a transition between locations and activities are available 2 = transition supports (e.g., visuals) are in place but not individualized to meet learner needs 3 = strategies for communicating when transitions will occur and the expected behavior are individualized to student needs

Figure 4.6. *(continued)*

- *Visual supports used to communicate expectations, rules, and directions.* These visuals include written words, pictures, objects, or even color-coding and should be individualized to meet the needs of each learner with ASD.

- *Individualized reinforcement to support behavioral or academic skill acquisition.*

- *Educators and other professionals offer students choices and honor these choices during the school day.* It is not uncommon that a choice might be offered ("Which book would you like to read?" or "What are you working for today?"), but the chosen item or activity is not delivered to the student as promised because of certain situational constraints. Item 11 should be scored "2" if some instructors honor students' choices, others do not, or if some students' choices are honored and others are not. If the staff does not offer choices at all, then Item 11 should be scored as "1" (not observed).

- *Well-structured transitions.* Transition supports are individualized to meet each learner's needs, and transitions occur quickly with minimal distractions. If students are observed independently making the transition between activities or environments, then score "0" (not applicable) for Item 13.

INSTRUCTIONAL CONSIDERATIONS

Instructional considerations is the second major category of the EBP COT and contains eight indicators focused on general strategies for organizing instruction to promote learning and independence across content. These indicators include instructional format (Indicator 13), clear instructional objectives (Indicator 14), activity schedules (Indicator 15), independent work systems (Indicator 16), other environmental supports (Indicator 17), systematic instruction (Indicator 18), direct instruction to support independence in academic and meaningful skills (Indicator 19), and three specific indicators related to staff behavior. These three staff behaviors include active staff participation in learning or classroom-related activities (Indicator 20), data collection (Indicator 21), and adult conversations directed toward students or academic activities (Indicator 22).

Instructional Format (Indicator 13)

The first instructional considerations indicator (Indicator 13) addresses the various types of instructional formats. Specific formats in the EBP COT include independent work and small-group, whole-group, or individual (e.g., one to one) instruction with an adult or peer.

Many configurations are possible, and there is no one right way for teaching students with ASD; some configurations may be better than others for certain content or skills, especially given the attention and memory challenges students with ASD face. Thus, if a student is not making progress or demonstrates limited engagement when participating in a specific learning format, then a team might ask if a different configuration could increase a student's learning.

The evidence regarding engagement and learning for students with ASD in various instructional formats is mixed (Carter, Cushing, Clark, & Kennedy, 2005; Ruble & McGrew, 2013; Steinbrenner & Watson, 2015). Student characteristics, teacher behavior, and environmental factors clearly influence engagement and learning. For example, Steinbrenner and Watson (2015) found that students with ASD were more engaged when teachers implemented student-directed instruction in small groups. Yet, this does not mean students with ASD should only participate in small groups. Rather, students can learn to participate in a variety of instructional contexts (Ruble & Robson, 2007). Some students may need systematic instruction to demonstrate engagement in a large-group setting, whereas other students may perform best in large groups. In both cases, students can likely develop the skills to actively participate in and learn from instruction delivered in different formats.

Instructional Objectives (Indicator 14)

Establishing clear instructional objectives is a well-documented instructional practice across grade levels. Instructional objectives not only serve as the overarching theme for instruction, but "when teachers communicate objectives for student learning, students can see more easily the connections between what they are doing in class and what they are supposed to learn" (Dean, Hubbell, Pitler, & Stone, 2012, p. 3). Yet, clearly articulating instructional objectives in comprehensible terms is an often overlooked practice for students with complex communication or behavioral challenges.

Chapter 1 described the cognitive profile in ASD. Difficulty understanding the big picture or gist of a topic or situation is one common characteristic of ASD. Clearly delineating the instructional objectives helps direct the attention of students with ASD to important concepts or ideas. In addition, students are better able to relate the new information to existing knowledge and store the information in ways they can access and use later when they understand what they are learning and why it is important. Thus, communicating instructional objectives or the big picture at the beginning of each lesson is critical. Although some students understand verbal purpose statements, others benefit from instructional objectives presented in writing or pictures.

Activity Schedules or Work Systems to Communicate Expectations During Group Instruction (Indicator 15) Activity schedules (also referred to as *work systems* when the concept of finished is represented) are similar to individual schedules because they are a visual representation of a sequence of activities. In the case of activity schedules, however, the visuals clearly indicate the specific activities embedded within a lesson or the sequence of instructional tasks. For example, a student with ASD might check his or her individual schedule that indicates a small-group math activity is next. Once the student arrives at the small-group lesson, the activity schedule contains the list of specific activities that will occur.

Activity schedules have been used to support individuals with ASD from childhood through adulthood and in many settings, including schools, homes, businesses, and communities. Similarly, activity schedules have been used to support academic and meaningful life skills. Knight and colleagues (2015) suggested that activity schedules can be considered a specific evidence-based practice when combined with systematic instruction.

Independent Work Systems to Communicate Expectations During Individual Tasks (Indicator 16) Indicator 16 addresses the use of independent work systems, which facilitate the completion of independent tasks for students with ASD (Carnahan, Hume, Clarke, & Borders, 2009). Regardless of structure, an independent work system uses visual and physical organization so tasks are clear and there is a systematic way to indicate completion. The overall organization communicates answers to four important questions: 1) What is the work? 2) How much work? 3) How do I know when I am finished? and 4) What do I do next? (Hume & Odom, 2007).

Independent work systems take various forms depending on the classroom and individual student needs. For example, an independent work system can be a stack of bins or drawers, binders with divider systems for organization, or even written lists clearly delineating the answers to the four questions previously listed. Regardless, the goal is to support learners with ASD in completing tasks independently. Although activity schedules and independent work systems share similar features and purposes, they are specifically delineated here to call attention to the need for clear organization during group and independent work times.

Additional Environmental Supports (Indicator 17) Environmental supports address the need many students with ASD have in directing their attention to the salient instructional materials and content. The environment can be set up in a way to direct students' attention by limiting distractions or organizing information in a way students can understand (Mesibov et al., 2005). Many of the supports previously discussed may overlap with or be considered in addition to Indicator 17. For example, first/then boards, visually represented directions, visual representations for token economies and choice, and video models are all examples of environmental supports that can be considered in this section but also apply in or overlap with other sections of the tool. The purpose of Indicator 17 is to call specific attention to the need that students with ASD have for support in addition to those areas already addressed. Tools such as timers, environmental arrangement of academic areas, use of peers as natural supports, and self-monitoring tools are all examples of environmental supports that may be intentionally placed in environments to aid students with ASD in functioning. Ultimately, teams might identify when a student has difficulty paying attention or demonstrating expected behaviors when scoring and discussing Indicator 17 and consider additional environmental supports that could be beneficial.

Systematic Instruction (Indicator 18) Strong evidence supports the use of systematic instruction for teaching students with ASD (Iovannone et al., 2003). Systematic instruction is a specific process that includes gaining the student's attention, providing a direction, waiting for a learner's response, and receiving feedback (error correction, reinforcement, or both) and can be applied to a variety of academic, social, or meaningful life skills. A systematic instructional approach often includes prompting, which can happen at different steps in the sequence. A prompt is an instructional cue used when teaching skills or when a student is learning to apply a skill in a new environment. A prompt is not a direction and is typically delivered just before or while a student performs a skill to increase the accuracy of a student's response (Neitzel & Wolery, 2010). Students with ASD may become dependent on prompts, especially if prompts are not systematically implemented or faded.

Many resources exist to support teachers in implementing systematic instruction for students with ASD (see the Resources section at the end of this chapter). A few important considerations include 1) clearly identifying the skills to teach, 2) developing and implementing a reinforcement system, and 3) carefully planning the prompting system. Although decisions regarding the specific types of prompts must be made by teams based on what they know about individual learners, some research suggests that students with ASD tend to respond better to most-to-least prompting systems or prompting systems in which learners receive more intrusive levels of prompts that are faded over time (Cengher et al., 2016).

Building Independence (Indicator 19) Indicator 19 addresses the significant challenges related to independent functioning that many individuals with ASD face (Hall et al., 2017; Hume, Loftin, & Lantz, 2009). Although students often acquire academic and life skills, especially when provided with systematic instruction using the processes briefly described in the previous section, they may find it difficult to perform these skills at school, at home, and in their communities (Hume, Boyd, Hamm, & Kucharczyk, 2014). Given these challenges, instruction to teach students with ASD to independently use academic and meaningful life skills in a variety of settings is an important component of the EBP COT. For example, a teacher might provide systematic instruction to teach students to develop a book report, organize homework or a school locker, wash their hands, or request help in an employment setting. It is important to remember that students with ASD need this systematic, targeted instruction to acquire skills before they are expected to demonstrate these academic and meaningful life skills independently. Following are a few points for building students' independent skill performance:

- *Systematically teach academic and meaningful life skills.* Consider reviewing the previous section specifically addressing systematic instruction and several of the resources at the end of the chapter. Again, it is important that a consistent teaching routine is in place to ensure students first acquire the academic and meaningful skills before expecting them to apply these in different environments.

- *Identify and create visual supports to increase the student's independent performance of acquired skills.* Many types of visual supports can promote independence, such as video models, visual directions, and activity schedules (Hume et al., 2014). Consider reviewing the information regarding visual supports in the Behavioral Supports section of this chapter.

- *Provide opportunities for the student to practice and monitor the acquired skills in many naturalistic settings.* Once students develop skills, they may need instruction to perform the skills independently in different, naturalistic settings (Neely et al., 2016). In addition, teaching students to monitor their performance of newly acquired skills can enhance their ability to perform these skills independently (Carr et al., 2014). Using visual supports, systematic prompting, and self-monitoring helps ensure students generalize and maintain their newly acquired skills in different environments.

Staff Behavior (Indicators 20, 21, and 22) The last three indicators in this section address staff behavior, including 1) staff actively participate with students in learning activities (Indicator 20), 2) staff actively collect data on student performance (Indicator 21), and 3) staff limit conversation to discussion directly related to curriculum, instruction, and classroom activities (Indicator 22). Although many educators likely agree these are important for promoting a positive classroom environment, creating a staff culture to support these behaviors can be challenging (Douglas, Chapin, & Nolan, 2015).

A few proactive steps can help ensure team members, especially those working together inside a classroom, are all on the same page (Carnahan, Williamson, Clarke, & Sorensen, 2009). First, consider developing a list of agreed-on values related to teaching students with ASD. Second, create and document clear guidelines or processes for implementing instruction (Douglas et al., 2015). These detailed descriptions can come in many forms but often follow a task analytic model and are written in protocol form. Finally, offer coaching and ongoing support to all team members. Individuals often demonstrate higher levels of fidelity when implementing systematic instruction when they receive coaching and verbal feedback (Cengher et al., 2016), and this can lead to better outcomes for students.

Scoring Instructional Considerations

The indicators described in the Instructional Considerations section are critical for all learners with ASD (see Figure 4.7). These strategies may look drastically different for individual learners, however, when they are implemented. The following should be present when observing instruction considerations:

- *Varied instructional configurations.* Assign a score of "3" if several areas are available for various instructional configurations (e.g., large group, small group, one to one) and more than one configuration is in use. Assign a score of "2" if the areas are available but only a single configuration is in use. *Note:* If the educator can easily describe how various configurations are used on a consistent basis, then consider returning to the classroom briefly to observe other configurations. Provide a score of "1" if only one configuration is available.

- *Clearly defined instructional goals and objectives presented in a way students with ASD understand.* Assign a score of "3" for this item if the teacher communicates the goals and objectives in a way that clearly aligns to the communication needs of the student (e.g., pictures, writing). Assign a score of "2" if the teacher states the objectives in a way that does not closely align to the students' communication needs. If you do not observe the beginning of the lesson, then consider asking the teacher to describe or show you how objectives were communicated.

- *Direct, systematic instruction to build independence with both functional and academic skills.* It is important to indicate if either or both functional or academic skills were addressed and the extent to which the professional used systematic instruction to teach a skill to independence.

- *Environmental supports to communicate expectations during instruction.* Assign a score of "3" if various supports are used to organize instruction. Assign a score of "2" if the supports are available but not used.

- *Activity schedules used within groups or centers.* Assign a score of "3" if activity schedules or work systems are used during instruction. Assign a score of "2" if the activity schedules or work system are available but not used.

- *Individualized independent work systems used to support work completion.* Assign a score of "0" if the EBP COT is completed during a time when the students are not engaged in independent work, but an independent work system is observed in the classroom. Assign a score of "2" if an independent work system is in use but does not address all four questions.

- *Instruction following the attention, direction, response, and feedback sequence, and often also including systematic prompting, especially to teach new skills or support students*

Figure 4.7. Scoring for instructional considerations.

Instructional Considerations		
Item	Examples	Scoring guidelines
13. Indicate the type(s) of instruction observed in the classroom during the observation Independent work Whole group Small group Individualized instruction with adult or peer Other (please describe):	Students rotate between small groups, independent work, and activities with peers during elementary centers time Students make the transition from a minilecture to individual work or lab activities during a high school science class	0 (N/A) = the teacher can articulate a reason this is not applicable in the observation setting, or a variety of instructional formats are not relevant to the observed instructional time (e.g., the observation takes place entirely during a one-to-one instruction session) 1 = one instructional format 2 = two instructional formats 3 = three or more instructional formats
14. Goals of instructional activities are clearly identifiable to observer without explanation	The goals of an instructional activity are written on the white board Visual supports provided to a student (e.g., picture symbol directions) indicate the goals of the task	0 (N/A) = the teacher can articulate a reason this is not applicable in the observation setting 1 = goals unclear or not stated 2 = educator briefly states goals but does not include rationale or importance of goals 3 = educator states goals at start of lesson, connects back to these throughout lesson, or posts goals
15. Activity schedules or work systems are used to communicate expectations including the activity to complete, amount required, and what will occur upon completion during all instructional activities	A student is expected to complete the steps in brushing his or her teeth. His or her schedule notes "brush your teeth." The necessary materials and step-by-step labels are at the sink (e.g., a toothbrush, toothpaste, the label "put toothpaste on toothbrush," a picture of the finished product) A student uses a written list of activities to complete at recess, including shooting 10 baskets at the basketball hoop, swinging on the swings for 5 minutes, asking a friend to throw a ball, and taking a 2-minute walk around the playground before lining up to go inside Students doing group work in a 12th grade English class are given a written checklist for their work task (e.g., create a group KWL chart, determine research assignments, make a plan for the next group meeting)	0 (N/A) = the teacher can articulate a reason this is not applicable in the observation setting 1 = no activity schedule or work system available 2 = a system is available, but neither the teacher nor student refer to it to monitor lesson progression 3 = a system is present, and the teacher and student refer to it to monitor lesson progression
16. Individualized work systems are used for independent work tasks to communicate activity to complete, how to complete, amount required and what will occur upon completion	Information is visually presented at a level students can understand (e.g., pictures, objects, written lists) A student uses a pocket folder in his or her sixth-grade class that organizes his or her work materials. The work that needs to be completed during independent work is in the left-hand pocket. The right-hand pocket is labeled "completed work." "Put the folder on Mrs. X's desk and choose a book from the library and read silently" is written on the back of the folder.	0 (N/A) = the teacher can articulate a reason this is not applicable in the observation setting, or independent work systems are observed in classroom but not applicable to observed instruction 1 = no system available, or the system is available but not used 2 = the system answers some, but not all, the questions by the system for individualized work

Figure 4.7. Scoring for instructional considerations.

	Instructional Considerations	
Item	Examples	Scoring guidelines
16. (continued)	A system of three stacked work bins labeled "1, 2, 3" is arranged on the left-hand side of a student's desk. A large bin is on the floor on the right-hand side of the desk. Three cards labeled "1, 2, 3" and one picture icon of a puzzle are on the desk. The student takes the "1" card from his or her desk and matches it to the one on the top bin on the left-hand side of the desk, completes the task inside the bin, and places the completed task in the bin on the right-hand side of the desk. This process repeats until all tasks in the bins are complete. The student then chooses a puzzle to put together.	3 = the system is organized to answer all the questions, and the student is able to use the system independently (or systematic prompting is in place to teach the student to use the system)
17. Additional environmental supports are embedded in classroom instruction *(check any of the following that were observed during instructional activities; mark any of the following that were observed in the classroom, but not used in instructional activities, with an "x")* 	Visual timers	
Token economy	
First/then instructions	
Graphic organizers	
Templates	
Visual directions	
Choice template (e.g., written list, picture icons)	
Video models	
Other (please describe):			A teacher reviews the schedule of activities for the entire class at the start of a writer's workshop session. After students move to their individual work stations, the teacher meets one to one with an individual learner to review the list of tasks for the child. He or she then sets a visual timer to remind the student how long the writing session will last. A 17-year-old young man is preparing for work. His teacher reviews the schedule of activities with him, including making the transition to the employment task, watching the video model, and then using a written visual schedule/checklist to complete the task. The student independently makes the transition to the employment setting and takes out his cell phone to watch the video model. He then opens a notebook with the specific steps to complete. There is a written comment at the top of the schedule that reads, "If you need help, then ask your supervisor."	0 (N/A) = the teacher can articulate a reason this is not applicable in the observation setting 1 = no environmental supports are observed in use in classroom instruction 2 = one to two environmental supports are observed in use in classroom instruction 3 = three or more environmental supports are observed in use in classroom instruction
18. Systematic instruction includes gaining attention, direction (prompting), student response, and feedback—either error correction or reinforcement	Teacher presented skills being taught, provided opportunities for practice, corrected errors or reinforced correct responses, provided repeated opportunities for generalization of skill areas, and assessed learner knowledge Staff asks a student "What is 3 multiplied by 3?" and the student responds, "6." The teacher says, "Good try. 3 multiplied by 2 equals 6. If 2 groups of 3 equals 6, what will we have if we add one more group of 3?" while demonstrating with counters.	0 (N/A) = the teacher can articulate a reason this is not applicable in the observation setting, or the observation occurs during a noninstructional time when the student is independent

Figure 4.7. *(continued)*

Instructional Considerations		
Item	Examples	Scoring guidelines
18. (continued)	A yellow card and a red card are on the table in front of a student. The staff says, "Give me the red card." The student takes the red card and puts it in the instructor's outstretched hand. The instructor says, "Great job! You gave me the red card," and immediately gives the student a preferred item. Nonexample: A teacher asks, "Who can tell me the name of the first president of the United States?" A student responds, "John Adams." The teacher says, "Anyone else?"	1 = systematic instruction should be used but is not, or several steps in the sequence are missing 2 = at least four steps in the process are clear and correctly implemented 3 = all components of systematic instruction are included and accurately implemented, and the process is individualized to meet learner needs
19. Classroom activities include direct instruction in building independence ☐ Meaningful skill independence ☐ Academic independence	Educator provides direct instruction on recording homework assignments in a planner to a student who neglected to turn in a homework assignment A student is taught the steps to make a peanut butter and jelly sandwich during one-to-one instruction	0 (N/A) = the teacher can articulate a reason this is not applicable in the observation setting, the observation occurs during a time when direct instruction is not appropriate, or the student is independent 1 = students are not required to complete tasks independently and are fully staff dependent 2 = the classroom activities emphasize either academic or life skill tasks without making a connection between academics and skills needed to be successful outside the classroom 3 = classroom instruction addresses both academic and life skills necessary for independence
20. Staff actively participate with students in learning or classroom-related activities (e.g., preparing materials)	Three staff members are in a classroom. While two staff members work directly with students, the other is in a "staff work area" sorting materials for independent work tasks.	0 (N/A) = the teacher can articulate a reason this is not applicable in the observation setting 1 = students are not engaged and in need of educator support or instruction 2 = some educators provided instruction, but other educators engaged in activities that distract learners or are not instructionally related 3 = all educators are actively and appropriately engaged in classroom-related activities
21. Staff are observed collecting data on student performance	Educator asks students to select a sample from their weekly math journals for their individual portfolios Educator records a student's responses on a prepared data sheet during one-to-one instruction Educator records anecdotal notes during a writing conference with a small group of students	0 (N/A) = the teacher can articulate a reason this is not applicable in the observation setting, or data collection not appropriate during this time 1 = educators are unaware of when data should be collected, or no data collection system available 2 = educators collect data on some goals and objectives but are unable to indicate a system for monitoring or using the data they collect 3 = educators actively collect student data
22. Conversation among staff limited to discussion directly related to curriculum, instruction, and classroom activities	As a teacher, speech-language pathologist, and paraeducator work collaboratively in a general education second-grade classroom to implement a lesson, they talk directly to the students about the social studies theme A student, his or her teacher, and someone from the employment site eat lunch together during their break at a vocational internship and discuss current events. The student uses his or her speech-generating device to make one- to two-word comments, and the teacher extends these comments by adding an additional word or two	0 (N/A) = the teacher can articulate a reason this is not applicable in the observation setting 1 = educators engage in high levels of off-topic or personal communication not directed to or including the learners 2 = educators mostly engage in child-directed, on-topic conversation 3 = educators focused on communication interactions with students; conversations related to classroom activities and used as opportunities to model or extend learner communication

Figure 4.7. *(continued)*

in generalizing skills from one environment to another. Item 19 should be scored a "3" (full implementation) if all the components of systematic instruction are observed. Provide a score of "2" (partial implementation) if any component is missing (e.g., teacher-provided feedback at the end of the interaction).

- *Adult behavior focused on student learning.* Adults engage with students when appropriate or in activities to support learning, such as material development and data collection. Adult discussion focuses on curriculum, classroom activities, or student needs.

COMMUNICATION CONSIDERATIONS

Communication is the final category of the EBP COT. This section is responsive to evidence that suggests that communication interventions, specifically functional communication training, is critical for many individuals with ASD (Fettig, 2013a; Sigafoos et al., 2009). Communication systems, whether verbal or in the form of AAC systems, are closely linked to social outcomes, academic engagement, and positive behavior for students with ASD (Watkins et al., 2015). Many students with ASD need direct, systematic instruction to use communication, no matter the mode. Whether a student is verbal, many individuals with ASD require daily, targeted communication instruction. Gaining access to resources, including the support of an SLP, may be necessary for creating well-developed communication systems that are designed to meet the needs of students with ASD. Educators can take valuable steps to promote communication, however, while waiting for such specialized support, five of which are addressed in the EBP COT.

Communication Indicators

Five indicators include observing for expressive communication systems (devices or tools that facilitate expressive communication for a student with ASD) in place, identifying how staff support students to use these systems, systematic instruction targeting communication across the day, social supports and instruction, and providing a variety of communication partners. This list is not intended to be exhaustive. Rather, these five indicators are meant to provide manageable steps special and general educators can take every day to increase the communication skills of students with ASD.

Communication Systems (Indicator 23)

It is essential that students with ASD, especially those who do not yet use verbal communication, have access to AAC systems accompanied by targeted instruction to learn to use the systems (National Research Council, 2001). Systems can come in different forms or modes from concrete objects to sign language to printed pictures or words or even voice output systems, such as those available on tablets or smart phones (Rowland, 2009; Van der Meer, 2014; Van der Meer & Rispoli, 2010; Wendt, 2009). Whatever the modality, students should be encouraged to use these systems across settings and individuals.

Selecting, designing, and teaching students to use communication systems can certainly be complicated. Mirenda (2009), Rubin (2017), and Watkins et al. (2015) described approaches teams can use to identify and select a variety of evidence-based practices to support social-communication. In addition, the Communication Matrix (https://communicationmatrix.org) can help school teams plan communication systems and opportunities. Despite the challenges, recognizing the need for communication systems and systematic instruction to teach communication is a critical starting point for supporting students with ASD.

Avoid Speaking for Students (Indicator 24) Adults and peers should encourage students with limited communication to use their communication systems. It is important to refrain from speaking on behalf of students. Instead, educators should use systematic instruction, including prompting and reinforcement, to teach students to communicate for a variety of purposes, including having their needs met, asking questions or gaining information, and engaging others socially.

Indicator 24 specifically reads, "Staff members do not speak on behalf of students and instead encourage and/or prompt students to use expressive communication." This can be challenging, however, if a student does not yet independently demonstrate communication. Several strategies can be helpful to avoid speaking for a student. For example, when the student is asked a question, an adult can make eye contact with the student, use a comment (e.g., "Oh, she asked about your lunch. Let's tell her what you ate"), and assist the student to touch a series of pictures or icons to comment (e.g., "I eat spaghetti. I not like"). Although there is certainly a level of assumption regarding whether the individual liked the food, these types of interactions put the student at the center of the conversation as an active and engaged participant. Web sites such as AssistiveWare Core Word Classroom (http://www.assistiveware.com/assistiveware-core-word-classroom) and Project Core (http://www.project-core.com) provide a variety of examples and resources for engaging students with significant challenges in communication interactions while avoiding the pitfall of speaking for the learner.

Embed Communication Instruction Throughout the School Day (Indicators 25 and 26) Indicators 25 and 26 are closely related when considering how to support communication development for students with ASD. Indicator 25 addresses embedding communication instruction throughout the day. A few important considerations include systematically teaching students to communicate and providing many opportunities for students to communicate. The first point addresses the need for "systematic effort to improve how individuals understand the communication of others and express themselves" (Brady et al., 2016, p. 127). This targeted communication instruction should occur throughout the school day and across instructional activities. Providing ample communication models is one important aspect of teaching students to communicate. Modeling is one way to provide students with access to a variety of communication purposes, the second consideration when planning communication instruction across the school day.

Communication occurs for a variety of purposes, all of which should be considered when planning interactions across the day. Having one's needs met or making basic requests are examples of these purposes. Communication instruction unfortunately often begins and ends with this purpose for many students with ASD (van der Meer et al., 2014). Individuals with ASD, including those with minimal verbal language, however, do communicate for a variety of purposes when provided with engaging opportunities (DiStefano, Shih, Kaiser, Landa, & Kasari, 2016). It is essential that communication instruction occur in engaging contexts and provide opportunities for students to communicate for purposes other than requesting, such as gaining information and social engagement.

Provide Opportunities to Communicate With Adults and Peers (Indicator 26) It is critical that students have opportunities to engage in naturalistic settings as they develop their communication skills (Beukelman & Mirenda, 2005), which includes opportunities to communicate with their peers and adults (Carter et al., 2005). Although adult–student interactions are important, engaging with peers is critical but often overlooked. Thus, providing access to same-age peers is another important consideration that can have classroom and schoolwide implications when embedding communication instruction throughout the day.

Educators often ask about strategies for building peer interactions for students with behavioral challenges or those with limited communication skills. Getting started can certainly be challenging; however, peer interactions are essential for promoting engagement (Carter et al., 2005, 2014; Mason et al., 2014). Several studies demonstrated increased engagement in students with ASD through the use of peers (Hochman, Carter, Bottema-Beutel, Harvey, & Gustafson, 2015; Ledford, Lane, Shepley & Kroll, 2016; McCurdy & Cole, 2014; Wolfberg, DeWitt, Young, & Nguyen, 2015). These increases have been shown in academic areas (McCurdy & Cole, 2014), social skills in the classroom and during less structured times (Ledford et al., 2016; Wolfberg et al., 2015), and across grade and age ranges (Hochman et al., 2015). Students with ASD may indicate higher interest in peers than in instructors; therefore, educators should utilize peer interactions to support increased engagement in tasks targeted for improvement with students with ASD.

Provide Targeted Social Skills Instruction (Indicator 27) Social skills instruction is another evidence-based practice for supporting students with ASD (Fettig, 2013b) that addresses the pervasive social-communication differences identified in many students with ASD (White, Koenig, & Scahill, 2007). This instruction can occur in groups or in individualized instruction, but the overall purpose should be to support students with ASD in developing meaningful social relationships and engaging successfully at home, at school, and in their communities (Carter et al., 2014).

A variety of social skills programs or curricula exist to support educators in developing targeted social-communication instruction. Assessing the specific needs of each individual learner, however, is essential for selecting the appropriate curricula. It may be necessary to identify the needs of each individual student and provide instruction targeted at those needs, rather than blindly implementing a packaged set of materials, for social skills instruction to be efficient and effective. This is not to say that packaged curricula are not valuable. Rather, educators must align the materials to the needs of the individuals participating in instruction.

Communication Scoring Considerations

It is important to note that a larger percentage of professionals who work with individuals with ASD indicate that they feel ill-equipped to support the development of expressive communication systems (Mirenda, 2001). If this is an area of challenge for the educators involved, then it is important to consider professional development opportunities to enhance practices in the communication domain.

Figure 4.8 describes examples and specific scoring information for the communication indicators. It is possible that some of the communication indicators may not be observable during a brief visit to a classroom. Detailed scoring considerations are described next:

- *Not all individuals with ASD require an expressive communication device.* Item 24 is critical for students who are nonverbal or who have some verbal skills but are developing a functional communication system. Score this section with a "0" if no students in the classroom require an expressive communication device. Score a "1" (not observed) if a student has a device but it is not being used across the instructional environment.

	Communication	
Item	Examples	Scoring guidelines
23. Communication systems (e.g., assistive technology) are utilized in the classroom to support students with communication differences	A student uses his or her voice output communication aid (VOCA) in a first-grade classroom. The first-grade teacher encourages the student to respond using his or her VOCA and allows the student time to navigate the device before responding. A student carries his or her picture exchange communication book throughout the building and uses the pictures to communicate with various staff members. Nonexample: A student who is nonverbal has no apparent means of communicating A VOCA sits on the student's desk, but he or she is not encouraged or instructed to use the device in the classroom, nor does he or she initiate use independently	0 (N/A) = all students have functional communication skills without the use of an aided communication system 1 = students have limited communication skills and no systems are available, or systems are available but not being used 2 = communication systems are available and are being used for some activities 3 = communication systems are available and are being used in a variety of activities
24. Staff members do not speak on behalf of students and instead encourage and/or prompt students to use expressive communication	A peer asks a child with ASD which color marker she would like to use; the teacher waits a few seconds and then provides a gesture prompt to cue the student to use her picture-based communication system to respond to the question.	1 = educators typically speak for the learner rather than encourage the learner to speak for him- or herself 2 = most educators encourage students to use their own communication systems, or they model appropriate communication responses for the learner 3 = students independently use communication systems, or all adults encourage students to use their systems to respond
25. Communication instruction is embedded throughout classroom activities	A teacher incorporates a student's speech-generating device (SGD) in vocabulary instruction When a student gives the teacher his or her glue and gestures for the teacher to open it, the teacher encourages him or her to use his or her words to request help A student uses his or her SGD to greet customers during a vocational internship	1 = limited clear, systematic communication instruction 2 = students have communication systems available but do not receive systematic or planned instruction to use them, or modeling or direct teaching occur but not a combination of both individualized modeling and direct teaching 3 = communication instruction is embedded through all academic, leisure, or social activities using modeling and systematic instruction at a level appropriate to each learner
26. Direct instruction in social interaction is embedded throughout classroom activities	A teacher watches a student take another student's pencil and uses the opportunity to provide instruction about asking permission before borrowing something. The teacher then notes the behavior to be addressed or taught during a one-to-one session the next day. A student leans over the student in the desk in front of him or her during independent work and says loudly, "Number 5 is wrong. So is number 9." The teacher quickly writes the student a note that explains that other students do not like to be corrected in front of the entire class, and all students should focus on their own work. The teacher practices the explicit skill of focusing on one's own work (not correcting others' work) during the daily review session at the end of the day. The teacher also adds the expectation to the student's "expected behavior" sheet in his notebook.	1 = limited teaching related to social skills, social-communication, or expected social behavior 2 = educators comment on social situations or behavior, but little direct and systematic teaching is available 3 = educators provide clear, systematic instruction regarding social behavior and social skills and implement supports (e.g., visual, written directions; video models) across the school day

Figure 4.8. Scoring considerations for communication.

Communication		
Item	Examples	Scoring guidelines
27. All students have opportunities to communicate with both peers and adults	Back-and-forth interactions with peers or staff are sustained by the student with ASD or a related disability beyond one exchange using a form of communication that is understood by communicative partners Staff model communication with and for students with limited functional communication using the system the student is learning to use Multiple opportunities are available for students to communicate with peers and adults (e.g., communicate with peers during small-group work, one-to-one communication with the teacher)	1 = few opportunities for students to communicate with adults and students, or adults are observed primarily talking to students rather than with students 2 = students have individualized communication systems available but few opportunities to use these systems 3 = students have opportunities throughout the day to talk with adults and other students using their individualized communication system, or adults model appropriate communication using the systems available to the students

Figure 4.8. *(continued)*

- *There might be inconsistencies related to Item 25 in some settings, particularly those in which multiple adults are in the room.* This indicator should be scored a "2" if some adults are encouraging students to use their devices and refrain from speaking on behalf of students.

- *The nature of instructional activities will affect which indicators in the communication section are observable.* For example, if students are engaged in independent work, then it is unlikely they will have many opportunities to practice social skills or interact with peers. In that circumstance, Items 27 (peers) and 28 (adults) should be marked "0" or "not applicable." Similarly, if students are engaged in student-directed group work, then they will likely have few opportunities to interact with adults, and Item 28 (adults) could be scored "0" as well.

SUMMARY

The EBP COT is a tool to support school leaders in building quality programming for students with ASD across the academic grades and content areas and across the continuum of educational settings. The purpose of the EBP COT is to serve as a catalyst for conversation and change; it is not intended as an evaluation tool. This chapter described a process for guiding observations and the specific components of the EBP COT. Remember, focusing on strengths and opportunities for growth is critical. Change does not happen overnight or all at once—prioritizing specific targets and providing the supports to help educators achieve these targets is critical for the successful use of the EBP COT.

ADDITIONAL RESOURCES

Web Sites

- AssistiveWare Core Word
  http://www.assistiveware.com/assistiveware-core-word-classroom

- Autism Internet Modules
  http://www.autisminternetmodules.org

- CAST
  http://www.cast.org

- Communication Matrix
  https://communicationmatrix.org
- National Center on Universal Design for Learning
  http://www.udlcenter.org
- National Professional Development Center on ASD
  http://autismpdc.fpg.unc.edu
- Program for the Education and Enrichment of Relationship Skills (PEERS)
  http://www2.semel.ucla.edu/peers
- Project Core
  http://www.project-core.com
- Universal Design for Learning Implementation and Research Network
  http://udl-irn.org

Recommended Reading

CAST. (2015). *What is UDL?* Retrieved from http://www.udlcenter.org/aboutudl/whatisudl

Collins, B. C. (2012). *Systematic instruction for students with moderate and severe disabilities.* Baltimore, MD: Paul H. Brookes Publishing Co.

Henry, S., & Smith Myles, B. (2013). *The comprehensive autism planning system (CAPS) for individuals with autism spectrum disorders and related disabilities: Integrative evidence-based practices throughout the student's day.* Shawnee Mission, KS: Autism Asperger Publishing.

Kabot, S., & Reeves, C. (2010). *Setting up classroom systems that support students with autism spectrum disorders.* Shawnee Mission, KS: Autism Asperger Publishing.

Kabot, S., & Reeves, C. (2012). *Building independence: How to create and use structured work systems.* Shawnee Mission, KS: Autism Asperger Publishing.

REFLECTION QUESTIONS

1. Reflect on the guiding steps for observations and describe how you might approach a teacher or school team to introduce the idea of the EBP COT.

2. List the three categories of the EBP COT. What are the indicators under each category?

3. Think about a learning environment such as an individual classroom in your school. Describe the areas in which you think the environment is strongest in terms of programming for students with ASD. What are the greatest opportunities for growth?

4. Reflect on the guiding steps for observations and describe how you would support a teacher or team after an observation. How will you approach the strengths and opportunities for growth? Describe how you could support the teacher in gaining access to any resources (e.g., knowledge development, professional development, materials, observing others) needed for improvement.

5. Examine the UDL framework located at http://www.udlcenter.org/aboutudl/udlguidelines. Align the individual considerations described in the environmental, instructional, and communication sections of this chapter with specific checkpoints on the UDL framework. Describe how you might promote teachers using the UDL framework to design educational settings that will support learners with ASD using this alignment.

5 Developing and Leading Collaborative School Cultures

Pamela Williamson, Christina R. Carnahan, and Sarah J. Letson

QUESTIONS THIS CHAPTER WILL ANSWER

1. What does the research say about developing collaborative school cultures?
2. How are evidence-based practices connected to larger concerns about providing school-based services to increasing numbers of students with ASD?
3. What is an action-oriented approach to building and sustaining collaborative school cultures? What steps can school leaders take to implement such an approach in a school setting?
4. What free evidence-based practice resources are available to build the capacity of stakeholders in knowledge, skills, and dispositions?
5. How can the EBP COT and Collaboration Guide be integrated in a larger systems-change framework?

School-age children and adolescents represent one of the largest populations of individuals with ASD in society (National Center for Health Statistics, 2013). This growing population represents an increase in responsibilities and challenges for school leaders regarding the day-to-day efforts to ensure compliance with federal mandates requiring high-quality education for all learners, including those with ASD (Pazey et al., 2014; Yell et al., 2005). In addition, school leaders face challenges such as 1) increased litigation, 2) parental demands for particular programs of instruction (e.g., applied behavior analysis [ABA]), and 3) limited knowledge among building leaders and teachers about ASD (Pazey et al., 2014).

Understanding specific evidence-based practices, such as those contained within the EBP COT, the process of evidence-based practice, and strategies for proactive problem solving, such as those in the Collaboration Guide described later in this chapter, are critical for managing and addressing the instructional needs and challenges of students with ASD in school settings. *Evidence-based practices* are defined as "specific focused intervention strategies that have evidence of efficacy" (Odom, Cox, Brock, & NPDC, 2013, p. 213) (see Chapter 3). Yet, evidence-based practice includes how educators and other professionals bring together what they know about evidence-based practice with what they know about their learners. Educators employ evidence-based practice when they use what they know about students' goals, students' history, and their professional judgment to inform how they implement evidence-based practices for individual learners (Odom et al., 2013; Smith, Schmidt, Edelen-Smith, & Cook, 2013). In spite of efforts to identify evidence-based practices from the research literature, gaps in the implementation for students with ASD have persisted. School leaders can serve as important change agents, moving best practice forward for all students, despite these challenges. Thus, the purpose of this chapter is to explore the role of school leaders and collaboration strategies that promote evidence-based practice by faculty and staff for students with ASD. It will specifically discuss how school leaders can use the EBP COT and Collaboration Guide as the foundation for promoting positive change.

LEADERSHIP FOR CHANGE IN PRACTICE

School leadership was largely absent from school reform agendas in the mid-2000s because teachers were seen as the change agents (The Wallace Foundation, 2013). Leithwood, Day, Sammons, Harris, and Hopkins (2008) noted that there is no evidence that a school has ever successfully changed its trajectory without a strong school leader. From more than 30 years of research on school reform, school leaders influence 1) the recruitment and retention of teachers (Darling-Hammond, LaPointe, Meyerson, Orr, & Cohen, 2007; Elliott & Clifford, 2014), 2) small but significant effects on student achievement (Elliott & Clifford, 2014; Louis, Leithwood, Wahlstrom, & Anderson, 2010), and 3) policy implementation at the school level. Perhaps most important, successful school leaders drive efforts to prepare schools to make way for change (Fullan, 1999, 2007; Waldron & McLeskey, 2010).

School Reform Research

A school's culture is defined by the beliefs and expectations that influence how a school system operates (Fullan, 2007). Improving the performance of faculty and staff using four basic leadership principles is the central task of school leaders (Leithwood et al., 2008), and they include 1) building vision and setting direction, 2) understanding faculty and staff personalities and attitudes, 3) creating collaborative cultures, and 4) managing teaching and learning programs. The following list provides a brief discussion of each of these concepts and the application to including individuals with ASD in schools and classrooms.

1. *Building vision and setting direction.* Building vision and setting direction includes efforts to develop and build faculty and staff motivation through shared vision. Shared goals are an important part of building a shared vision. Fostering faculty and staff acceptance of established goals and creating an environment of high expectations is essential. Leaders might focus on the importance of social and academic inclusion for all learners with ASD, including those with

very complex communication and behavioral challenges, when developing systemwide goals. Another shared goal might address high academic standards, or the expectation that all students can and will learn and make progress during the school year. Having high expectations and believing they are capable of learning is essential for students across the autism spectrum. The EBP COT could be used to establish goals at the classroom level. For example, a school leader and small group of teachers could meet to establish shared goals after conducting an observation and self-assessment.

2. *Understanding faculty and staff personalities and attitudes.* Critical dispositions related to changing practice include commitment (motivation for teaching and change), resilience (ability to respond flexibly in the face of challenge and change), and capacity (Leithwood et al., 2008). Successful leaders understand their faculty and staff, including their personalities, dispositions, and attitudes, as well as how these influence the school climate. They also attend closely to faculty and staff strengths and opportunities for development. School leaders might consider faculty and staff commitment, or buy-in, to the importance of evidence-based practices for improving outcomes. Similarly, school leaders should consider teacher capacity for implementing evidence-based practices in classrooms. For example, once a team has identified areas of strength and need using the EBP COT, a school leader might determine what the teacher already knows about specific evidence-based practices and, more important, how and when to use them. School leaders can use the EBP COT as a guide to determine the strengths and needs of teachers and create opportunities for professional development through study groups, coaching from others, or even formal professional development (e.g., conferences, workshops). School leaders consider staff resilience, or how staff will respond when an evidence-based practice is used and is not initially successful; planning supports for teachers and staff to ensure persistence in determining why the practice was not successful, how to make it work, or the selection of a different practice is critical.

3. *Creating collaborative cultures.* Successful leaders build collaborative cultures that promote productive relationships internally and externally with families and the larger community (McLeskey & Waldron, 2010). Working with families is the cornerstone of special education, particularly for families of students with ASD. It is important to involve students' families in critical decisions that affect their children. Family members should also be assured that their opinions are valued and their input is welcome, regardless of the nature of their feedback (i.e., positive, critical). Successful avenues are cultivated for information sharing and problem solving by establishing these relationships. Using the EBP COT can help school teams identify specific opportunities for engaging families. For example, if the team identifies functional communication as an important area for growth, then family input can drive what the system looks like and how it is implemented. Similarly, if reinforcement is an area of need, then families can provide insight into items or activities that are especially interesting to the individual with ASD.

4. *Managing teaching and learning programs.* Successful leaders manage the teaching and learning programs in their buildings through 1) careful staff selection, 2) instructional support, 3) data monitoring, and 4) buffering faculty and staff

from distractions from their work (Leithwood et al., 2008). Selecting staff that are open and flexible to learning about new practices is key. Building leaders need to determine support needs (e.g., additional training, including coaching) and the extent to which current progress monitoring efforts reflect data sufficient to evaluate if evidence-based practices capture movement in student outcomes. Finally, building leaders should consider sheltering instructional staff from other school initiatives while they are in the midst of implementation.

Models for School Change

Odom and his colleagues (2013) suggested that **innovation science** might provide insight into systematic ways to ensure more schools use evidence-based practices for students with ASD. Because evidence-based practices are an educational innovation, Fixsen, Blase, Naoom, and Duda (2013–2015) developed an implementation model for education that articulated critical drivers of innovation. **Implementation drivers,** or factors that influence the implementation of evidence-based practices, include competency (i.e., selection of personnel, professional development, coaching, performance assessment/fidelity), organization (i.e., decision/support data systems, facilitative administration, systems interventions), and leadership (i.e., technical, adaptive) (Fixsen et al., 2013–2015).

Others have studied **improvement science** as a way to move educational research into practice (Bryk, Gomez, & Grunow, 2010; Lewis, 2015). Hypothesizing that much of the reason evidence-based practices have not found their way into schools has to do with understanding what knowledge is needed and under what circumstances (Lewis, 2015; Smith et al., 2013). Scholars from this perspective acknowledge that evidence-based practices are developed with support from researchers in ideal conditions (Smith et al., 2013). As such, evidence-based practices represent the "basic knowledge" that is contained in the intervention that was developed and initially implemented under ideal circumstances (Lewis, 2015, p. 54). Improvement models anticipate that enacting evidence-based practice requires profound knowledge that includes the generalizable knowledge of evidence-based practices (i.e., knowledge in the program) and organizational-specific knowledge (i.e., knowledge in the people and system). Profound knowledge is local and related to implementing interventions with students in authentic contexts. Implementation is focused on making adjustments to ensure the evidence-based practices function well in the context in which they are deployed. Notably, this is consistent with the approach of some scholars who recommend starting an intervention as designed and making adjustments as needed to suit individual students and the context (e.g., Mirenda, 2003; Pressley, 2002).

STRATEGIES FOR DEVELOPING AND SUSTAINING COLLABORATIVE CULTURES TO SUPPORT EVIDENCE-BASED PRACTICES

Drawing from the school reform literature and school change models, leadership practices and activities should be aimed at developing and sustaining collaborative cultures to facilitate the use of evidence-based practices for students with ASD. Collaborative cultures encourage open, transparent discussion that emphasizes thoughtful risk taking and problem solving. More important, collaborative cultures support the development of knowledge, skills, and dispositions to build the capacity of faculty and staff to implement and sustain evidence-based practices for students with ASD. Successful leaders of change draw from the following practices to lead change efforts:

- Develop the motivation of faculty and staff for change by deciding on a shared vision.
- Determine the extant capacity of personnel for implementation of evidence-based practices.
- Organize systems to accommodate change and collaboration among teachers, paraeducators, related services personnel, families, and students.
- Use data to systematically build the capacity of stakeholders.
- Use collaborative professional development practices that include professional development, coaching, and development of dispositions for change.
- Select high-quality personnel through collaborative behavioral interviewing.

Setting the Stage for Change

The section below addresses each of the critical factors related to positive school culture and developing the foundation of quality programming for individuals with ASD. Alone, each of these considerations is important, but together, they provide a clear organizational structure in which school teams can affect important change.

Vision and Direction School leaders can use the EBP COT to build a shared vision and set the direction of stakeholders to support, develop, and sustain the use of evidence-based practices for students with ASD. Challenges to this vision might include lack of knowledge about the practices included in the EBP COT, the importance of these for promoting positive outcomes of students with ASD and their families, and the use of unsubstantiated interventions and claims that are readily made to the public (Mayton, Wheeler, Menendez, & Zhang, 2010). Additional challenges might include school structures that make data gathering and sharing difficult, such as limited use of technology or even mistrust of leadership. Determining the current **school culture** and what might be needed to increase collaboration is an important first step for promoting change.

Capacity of Personnel Effective leaders are keen observers of systems and personnel. Systematically, they identify potential facilitators and challenges to embedding evidence-based practice for students with ASD in buildings. For example, they take time to determine who in the building already knows about the practices outlined in the EBP COT. Of those individuals, they determine who might have influence over their peers and who might be able to build the capacity of their colleagues as teacher leaders, mentors, or coaches. They also identify teachers and others who might need additional support to develop the knowledge, skills, and dispositions to effectively use the practices to facilitate student outcomes.

Organize Systems for Change Conducting an analysis of existing systems to determine what might facilitate or present challenges to schoolwide implementation of evidence-based practice for students with ASD must be considered. For example, is the school schedule amenable to providing collaborative time for planning, implementing, and evaluating the progress toward the schoolwide use of evidence-based practice? Can regularly scheduled meetings be aligned to better use time to improve practice? How will the EBP COT be used to identify actionable steps? The result of data gathering should include improvements that accommodate change and collaboration among teachers, paraeducators, related services personnel, families, and students.

Communication and Dispositions of Effective Leaders Although the EBP COT can provide teams with a starting point for increasing their use of evidence-based practices, clear communication is an essential aspect for change. Use the EBP COT Collaboration Guide (see Figure 5.1) as a tool for facilitating problem solving after observations and self-assessment. The Collaboration Guide is designed to promote honest, forward-focused conversations, create a concrete list of action items, and plan for necessary resources and follow up. The remainder of the chapter discusses how the EBP COT and Collaboration Guide can be used to promote problem solving and collaborative planning.

Challenges will occur along the way, despite careful planning, and successful leaders must adapt to meet these challenges. Drawing from the work of Heifetz, Grashow, and Linsky (2009), Fixsen, Blase, Van Dyke, and Metz (n.d.) developed a list of communication strategies and dispositions that have been adapted to facilitate conversations and promote positive, collaborative cultures.

- *Step into the fray and develop deeper understanding of the conflict.* Reframe conflict as an opportunity for growth during implementation of evidence-base practice. From the improvement science perspective, systematic analysis of problems might lead to development of the people and systems that are using evidence-based practice because implementation in buildings is different from ideal implementations of evidence-based practices by researchers (Lewis, 2015). It is essential the school leaders clearly understand the purpose in using the EBP COT. Some teams may use the tool for ongoing self-evaluation, improvement, and proactive problem solving. Others, however, may have experienced a challenge or concern that was the impetus. In either case, developing a deep understanding of the situation is essential.

- *Put the unspoken issues on the table.* It is critical for leaders to address threats to providing evidence-based practices for all students with ASD by naming and discussing the issues openly. It is likely they are already being discussed, although unproductively. The school leaders should use the Collaboration Guide to facilitate an honest conversation, even if uncomfortable, about the rationale for using the EBP COT. Rather than merely presenting or hearing a concern, encourage team members to elaborate on concerns and present possible solutions. These types of candid discussions can lead to problem solving, information sharing, and even myth busting.

- *Create a safe environment where diversity of thought is valued and cultivated.* Innovation flourishes when everyone is actively thinking about how to improve outcomes for students with ASD. The Collaboration Guide is designed to encourage teams to select one or two specific areas for growth at a time. It is particularly important to have open communication across stakeholder groups when determining which area on the EBP COT should be prioritized. In addition, hearing the perspectives of all team members can promote creative problem solving when identifying the action items and resources and determining who is responsible.

- *Regulate the stress of others.* Hoppey and McLeskey (2013) conducted a case study of an effective principal and found that shielding faculty from unnecessary burdens was highly valued by school personnel. Thus, school leaders should consider strategies for ensuring the teacher (or whomever is most responsible for implementing the action plan) feels supportive and is not overwhelmed. For example, support staff such as paraeducators can help with material preparation, and related services professionals can provide in-depth training or support for implementing a new intervention or system.

Collaboration Guide

Reason for observation/meeting:
(Discuss specific reasons for using the guide)

Setting:
(Where the observation occurs)

Date:
Observer(s):
(List observers and indicate if self-assessment occurred)

Strengths:
(List two to three areas of strength)

Opportunities for growth:
(List one or two specific areas or items for growth)

Specific next steps:
(What needs to happen? Who is responsible? What resources are needed?)

Step	What needs to happen?	Who is responsible?	When will it happen (deadlines)?	Resources needed (list web site, person)
1.				
2.				
3.				

Follow up:
(Who will follow up and when?)

Success measures:
(How will we know we were successful or met our goals?)

Step	How will we know we were successful or met goal?	When will we decide?	Outcome
1.			

Figure 5.1. EBP COT Collaboration Guide.

Facilitating Evidence-Based Practice for Students with ASD: A Classroom Observation Tool for Building Quality Education
by Christina R. Carnahan and K. Alisa Lowrey. Copyright © 2018 by Paul H. Brookes Publishing Co., Inc. All rights reserved.

- *Maintain disciplined attention.* Effective leaders continuously monitor systems and personnel to look for signs of trouble. School leaders can plan for periodic observations of or check-ins with faculty and staff. In addition, determining what success will look like (i.e., How will we know we were successful or met our goal?) during the planning process promotes feelings of success from the start. Identifying and addressing issues early and planning specific action steps are critical for student success and possible prevention of similar issues in the future.

Sustaining Change

After leaders have successfully set the stage for change and established the new school climate, they have to maintain these changes over time. Leadership should implement four activities to more easily proceed through this second process—practicing leadership, using data to inform decisions, providing opportunities for collaborative professional development, and recruiting quality personnel moving forward. Sustaining change is an ongoing process, and these activities should be revisited periodically to ensure they are functioning effectively.

Distributed Leadership No one leader can know or do all things (McLeskey & Waldron, 2002). Collaborative cultures have increased needs for leadership from other school personnel (Mangin, 2007). Thus, one common strategy is the use of **distributed** (or shared) **leadership** and decision making. Benefits of distributed leadership include collaborative decision making and problem solving. It gives those closest to the work the ability to affect that work. In addition, it gives others the ability to raise needed questions to improve what happens for students with ASD and their families. Leadership teams might include ad hoc groups organized specifically to support the use of approaches outlined in the EBP COT or standing committees, such as teams of special education teachers, general education teachers, or others tasked with making collaborative decisions, problem solving, and sustaining professional development on a regular basis.

Use of Data Using data to support professional development is a critical yet underemployed approach to systems change (Waldron & McLeskey, 2010). Variations in how professionals implement evidence-based practices are "important sources of information" for school leaders (Lewis, 2015, p. 55). For example, the success of strategies such as visual schedules or systematic prompting is directly related to how these strategies are matched to individual student need and then actually implemented. A visual schedule may be ineffective if it does not align to an individual student's level of understanding or he or she is not systematically taught to use the schedule. Similarly, if a set of prompts is used during math instruction for a student but does not actually match with the student's need, then it is unlikely the student will learn the concept. Thus, gathering data about how evidence-based practices are implemented should inform systematic capacity building efforts. School leaders could use data to create miniworkshops before school or even online to increase implementation accuracy.

Plan-do-study-act (PDSA) cycles (Lewis, 2015) is one tool suggested in the literature to develop actionable data. PDSA cycles are guided by three questions: 1) What are we trying to accomplish? 2) How will we know that a change resulted in improvement? and 3) What change can we make that will result in improvement? These concepts are embedded within the Collaboration Guide and should guide school-based teams charged with developing, sustaining, or evaluating some aspect of implementation.

Collaborative Professional Development Although research dispels the idea that high-quality professional development alone can influence teachers' implementation of evidence-based practices in their classrooms, didactic knowledge and early practice in a safe environment form the foundation for learning (Joyce & Showers, 2002). Ensuring teachers, paraeducators, and other related services professionals have access to high-quality professional development is critical for implementation of evidence-based practices for students with ASD.

Able, Sreckovic, Schultz, Garwood, and Sherman (2015) conducted a study with general and special education teachers to determine what teachers felt they needed to help students with ASD in their classrooms. Teacher needs included access to 1) information about ASD and the characteristics of individual students, 2) efficacious interventions to address academic and social needs, 3) facilitation of social needs, and 4) promotion of advocacy. High-quality resources are available to help instructional staff develop knowledge in these areas.

High-quality resources available on the web include modules on a variety of topics. For example, the Autism Internet Modules (AIM) web site offers 45 modules available with 25 additional modules in development available at http://www.autisminternet modules.org. Also, the NPDC offers practice guides (http://autismpdc.fpg.unc.edu/national-professional-development-center-autism-spectrum-disorder) for most of the identified evidence-based practices, and they include summaries of the salient features of the evidence-based practice (e.g., what it is, who it can be used for, setting information, step-by-step directions, fidelity monitoring tools) as well as a review of the evidence that supports the practice. Identifying which of these specific resources a teacher or team needs and how the resources will be accessed is an essential aspect of the Collaboration Guide.

In addition to providing individual teachers and small groups access to resources, principals and other leaders could systematically introduce information to the staff during a regularly scheduled meeting (e.g., faculty meeting, community of practice meetings). Modeling and practice are critical features that should be part of these introductory meetings. Modeling could include teachers modeling the process for their peers or video models from the web (e.g., discrete trial teaching videos from YouTube). Finally, developing a scenario that could be used for role play would provide teachers the opportunity to practice what they observed being modeled, albeit in an artificial way.

As a follow-up to high-quality professional development, coaching from school leaders, peer mentors (i.e., other teachers), or even a curriculum specialist can help teachers rehearse skills while they are in the acquisition phase. Thus, specific action steps should incorporate opportunities for modeling and coaching on a regular basis. In a seminal meta-analysis, Joyce and Showers (2002) demonstrated that only 5% of teachers used what they learned in their classrooms, even with high-quality professional development that included modeling, practice, and feedback. Adding a coaching component, or a component that promoted reflection and collaboration among teachers, increased the number of teachers who implemented what they learned to more than 80%. Building teacher confidence (McCray & McHatton, 2011), increasing fidelity of implementation (Fixsen et al., 2013–2015), and developing the skills of new hires who may have missed initial professional development are additional benefits of coaching.

Coaches also require professional development. Hall (2015) suggested that having access to a community of practice for coaches is important, which might be a way to use outside consultants or coaches. Experts could build the capacity of coaches.

Leithwood and his colleagues (2008) noted the importance of developing dispositions for change. Part of this might include personal reflection regarding strengths and opportunities for growth, or what Wheatley called being "willing to be disturbed" (2002, p. 38). When teachers and others believe what they are doing already helps children, their beliefs and ideas may need to be challenged in safe exchange. Reflection is critical to leaving people available and curious about learning new information.

Selecting Personnel In addition to developing personnel, hiring new personnel with the knowledge, skills, and dispositions consistent with collaborative cultures is critical. Leithwood and his colleagues (2008) noted that recruiting and retaining personnel greatly influences the success of schools. Students with ASD come into contact with many school personnel, including special and general education teachers, paraeducators, and related school personnel; thus, it is critical for principals to recruit high-quality faculty and staff. Fixsen and his colleagues (2013–2015) described the ideal hiring situation as a mutual process. Examination of potential candidates' knowledge, skills, and dispositions should be explored, with specific attention to the evidence-based practices outlined in the COT.

Also, leaders should consider a team-based approach to interviewing top candidates because it is the team that serves students with ASD. Teams would ideally include individuals who would be working together. Given the close proximity to the work environment, teams could provide important insight into critical dispositions needed to work in particular contexts and with particular students with ASD. A standard list of interview questions or an interview guide could be developed.

Using behavioral instead of traditional interview questions improves the likelihood of selecting the best candidate for the job (Hoevemeyer, 2006). Based on the notion that past behavior predicts future behavior, behavioral interviewing techniques have been around for decades (Hoevemeyer, 2006). Traditional interviews often use what-if scenarios, whereas behavioral interviews ask potential candidates to provide an example of a time when they encountered a job-related situation. Behavioral interview questions are structured using a method that asks candidates to describe the *s*ituation, *t*ask, *a*ction, and *r*esult, or the **STAR method.** For example, instead of asking, "How do you ensure you are knowledgeable about research-based strategies?" A team member might ask, "Tell me about a time when you used data to change your practice for a student with ASD. Describe the situation, the task you were working toward, the action you took, and the result of that action."

SUMMARY

Decades of research on school reform suggest that developing collaborative school cultures is critical to changing and sustaining schools. Implementation and improvement models support additional techniques for ensuring fidelity of implementation of evidence-based practices for students with ASD. From this work, strategies were given to set the stage for change (i.e., developing vision and direction, evaluating the capacity of personnel, organizing systems for change) using the EBP COT and sustained change (i.e., systematic data collection and sharing, collaborative professional development, selecting personnel) using the Collaboration Guide.

ADDITIONAL RESOURCES

- Active Implementation Hub
  http://implementation.fpg.unc.edu
  Modules, lessons, activities, and short courses. The Active Implementation Hub is a free, online learning environment for use by any stakeholder involved in active implementation and scaling up of programs and innovations. The site goal is to increase the knowledge and improve the performance of persons engaged in actively implementing any program or practice.

- Association for Science in Autism Treatment
  http://www.asatonline.org/research-treatment/resources/videos
  Contains four video demonstrations

- Autism ABA curriculum
  http://www.autismabacurriculum.com/programs
  Provides 170 programs in 12 categories to help develop specific skills for students with ASD using ABA

- Autism Speaks
  http://www.autismspeaks.org
  Tools for professionals lists available resources, including instructional techniques, ABA, and general ASD instruction

- Brining ABA
  http://www.bringingaba.com
  Offers continuing education courses, readings, sample lessons, and training for using ABA for students with ASD

- NPDC
  http://autismpdc.fpg.unc.edu
  Provides evidence-based guides

- Ohio Center for Autism and Low Incidence and Autism Internet Modules
  http://www.autisminternetmodules.org
  Has 45 modules available and 25 additional modules in development

- Partington Behavior Analysts
  http://www.partingtonbehavioranalysts.com/page/workshops-and-seminars-20.html
  Provides professional development workshops for ABA with students with ASD

- Wong et al. (2015)
  http://autismpdc.unc.edu/sites/autismpdc.fpg.unc.edu/files/2014-EBP-Report.pdf
  Evidence-based practices for children, youth, and young adults with ASD

A series of ABA videos that demonstrate a step-by-step process of describing ABA components in five chapters—discrete trial, reinforcement, prompting, generalization, and incidental teaching
- https://www.youtube.com/watch?v=7pN6ydLE4EQ
- https://www.youtube.com/watch?v=crFjZlWWZo0
- https://www.youtube.com/watch?v=TDijJjKHMVQ
- https://www.youtube.com/watch?v=xU395HgXl2s
- https://www.youtube.com/watch?v=yzgC9ZPzot8

REFLECTION QUESTIONS

1. How prepared is your school to implement evidence-based practices? How do you know?

2. Who are the leaders in your building? Who might be ready to help develop the capacity of their colleagues?

3. How can you begin to use the EBP COT and corresponding Collaboration Guide in your school?

4. What school culture factors might facilitate the process? What barriers might you face?

5. What external resources might be helpful, including parent groups and others?

6. How consistent are your current practices to develop the knowledge, skills, and dispositions of your building personnel with collaborative professional development practices?

7. How will you help your building sustain implementation in the event you leave the building?

Appendix

Development of a Standardized Benchmark Assessment Tool to Facilitate EBP for Students With ASD

Christina R. Carnahan
University of Cincinnati

Alisa Lowrey
University of Southern Mississippi

Kate Snyder
Springfield College

Abstract: The purpose of this paper is to describe the development of an accessible, standardized benchmark assessment (i.e., the Evidence Based Practice Classroom Checklist [EBP CC]) to support administrators, school leaders, and educators in collaborative implementation of evidence-based practices for students with autism spectrum disorder (ASD). This series of studies occurred in three phases across two states. The first phase was design and content validity testing. The second phase was testing of the implementation process in schools including reliability assessments. Finally, the third phase addressed implementation on a larger scale and evaluation. Results indicated the EBP CC was a valid tool that represented the foundational practices necessary for students with ASD. Administrators found such a tool important and necessary. Additionally, results indicated reliability in measuring evidence-based practices used in classrooms. Implications for research and practice are discussed.

The number of students with autism spectrum disorder (ASD) served in public schools has steadily been on the rise (Wong et al., 2014). At the same time, The No Child Left Behind Act (NCLB) of 2001 and the reauthorization of the Individuals with Disabilities Education Act (IDEA) in 2004 have called educators to action, suggesting all teachers, including those serving students with ASD, must utilize effective, evidence-based practices (EBP) (Jones, 2009). In response, researchers have made considerable efforts to delineate what constitutes an EBP (Cook, Tankersley, & Landrum, 2009) and to disseminate the information to educators and other professionals through efforts such as the Autism Internet Modules (AIM).

Educators are expected to select these EBPs by bringing together knowledge about the practices and the needs of their specific students (Odom, Boyd, Hall, & Hume, 2010). Unfortunately, availability does not equate to use (McLeskey & Billingsly, 2008; Simpson, 2005). Implementation of these EBPs with the frequency or rigor outlined in legislation remains low (Burns & Ysseldyke, 2009; Cook & Schirmer, 2003). The development of EPB tools that diminish barriers and facilitate effective and efficient implementation for teachers and administrators is necessary to bridge the gap between research and practice.

IMPLEMENTING EBPS IN SCHOOLS

Teachers indicate three primary barriers to their use of EBP in the classroom: time, access, and a lack of confidence in analyzing research (Williams & Coles, 2007). These barriers are especially understandable in the field of ASD, where the continuing increase in prevalence has caused the education system to be flooded with information about potential interventions, many of which lack effectiveness data (Simpson, 2004). When teachers do not have the time, access, and confidence to analyze the multitude of strategies available, they may implement non–evidence-based strategies or implement EBPs poorly.

Access and Confidence

To support teachers in identifying which strategies in the field of ASD have a sound evidence-base, two national groups developed resources to help determine and disseminate information. The National Professional Development Center on Autism Spectrum Disorders (NPDC on ASD) and the National Autism Center (NAC) both published reports to inform educators and parents about evidence-based practices. The NPDC on ASD published briefs on evidence-based practices identified through their work (2010, 2014). In 2010, 24 practices were identified. In 2014, these EPB were updated to include 27 practices. The EBP briefs provide an overview of the practice, a guide to the steps of implementation, an implementation checklist, and information detailing the evidence base for each practice. The NAC also published a report on their National Standards Project (2009) that identified established (11), emerging (22), and unestablished (5) treatments for students with ASD. The report details the criteria for establishing treatments, describes each of the treatments and its supporting evidence, and makes recommendations about how the treatments should be implemented. These two national projects address educators' concerns about their ability to critically evaluate educational research. Although very useful in discerning which practices are evidence based, teachers also indicate time constraints influence their use of EBP (Williams & Cole, 2007).

Time

These concerns about time are an important consideration in the development of resources designed to support classroom practices. Time- related issues impact a teacher's ability to implement quality instructional practices and can be a significant source of job frustration (Billingsley, 2010). Simpson and colleagues (2011) suggested that qualified teachers of students with ASD should be knowledgeable about EBP and should have extensive experience in applying these practices to learners with varying levels of need.

However, many teachers of students with ASD do not receive intensive preservice training or professional development about the disorder. Thus, it is not surprising that implementing EBP for these learners can feel time consuming for several reasons.

General and special education teachers with little knowledge of autism may not be aware of the NPDC or the EBP briefs. Lack of awareness could translate to substantial time searching for EBP. Second, awareness of EBP does not necessarily equate to knowledge or experience of how to actually implement practices. Thus, some educators may know there are specific EBP for serving students with ASD, but without previous experience implementing these practices, may invest substantial time studying the practice and determining the steps necessary for specific settings. Finally, if educators are aware of the EBPs and resources for gaining additional information regarding these practices but lack experience in using these to meet individual needs, additional time may be needed to determine how to individualize each practice to meet the unique needs of students.

Supporting Systemic Implementation of EBP in Schools

Given the ongoing challenges of translating research to practice, recent focus has shifted to factors that influence systemic implementation of EBPs, or implementation science (Cook & Odom, 2013). Odom and colleagues (2010, 2013) described five aspects of implementation models including collaborative planning by stakeholders, high-quality materials, technical support, stakeholder readiness, and contextual considerations. In order for implementation to be effective, much of the implementation science research describes important state-level processes dependent on both top-down and bottom-up activities (Odom, Duda, Kucharczyk, Cox, & Stabel, 2014).

Many classroom teachers, administrators, and other school leaders are often waiting for these efforts to make their way into districts, school buildings, and classrooms. While state- and district-level processes are critical (Klingner, Boardman, & McMaster, 2013), an administrator or school leader can be the impetus for change. In fact, an administrator or other school leader who actively supports the use of EBP is also critical in increasing the use of these practices in our schools (Domitrovich et al., 2008; Rohrbach, Grana, Sussman, & Valente, 2006). Thus, if an administrator/leader has the necessary knowledge and resources and supports teachers in learning about and using these resources, chances are greater that all students, including those with ASD, will receive evidence-based instruction.

There are several comprehensive assessment and planning resources that administrators/leaders and classroom teachers can use to guide their assessment, planning, and implementation of EBP, such as the Louisiana Autism Quality Indicators (LAQI) (Lowrey et al., 2010) or the Tier 1 Classroom Checklist-ASD Nest Program (Bleiweiss, Hough, & Cohen, 2013). However, the processes are sometimes extensive and could be perceived as daunting, especially for classroom teachers and administrators/leaders who are frequently overburdened with paperwork, lack of ASD related training, and other administrative challenges.

Development of a Benchmark Assessment Tool

Developing a short, standardized benchmark assessment tool is one strategy that may improve the implementation of EPB practice for students with ASD. Since NCLB (2001), benchmark assessments have been widely used throughout the school year as a way to measure student progress between formative and state assessments (Olson, 2005a; Olson, 2005b). They are typically quick assessments that provide a snapshot of students' abilities on identified skills and targets (Herman, Osmundson, & Dietel, 2010; Olson, 2005a). These benchmark assessments include scoring and administration procedures that maintain validity and reliability in measurement (California Department of Education, n.d.). Creating a similar standardized benchmark assessment, focused on classrooms rather than students, based on the unified EPB from both the NSP and the NPDC-ASD for administrators/leaders, general, and special educators could possibly address some of the previously mentioned barriers. Two fundamental questions are posed: 'What are the necessary components of a benchmark assessment tool designed to support administrators, other school leaders, general, and special educators in implementing EBP for students with ASD?' and 'Given competing agendas and differences in background experience, can a variety of stakeholders assess the use of these EBP with the same tool?'

The purpose of this paper is to describe a series of studies detailing the development of the EBP Classroom Checklist (EBP CC) for Educators for use in both general and special education classrooms serving students with ASD. This series of studies had several goals: (a) establish the content validity of the instrument through a content analysis design, (b) determine the interrater reliability of the benchmark assessment tool when used in a classroom environment by multiple raters, and (c) determine the satisfaction of users upon broader implementation.

Method

The initial design and validation of the EBP CC occurred in three phases. Phase 1 was Design. Phase 2 was Implementation and Modification. Phase 3 was Implementation and Evaluation. Each Phase is described below. Phase 1 and 2 took place in one state while Phase 3 was implemented in a different state. Institutional Review Board approval was secured for all phases of study.

PHASE 1: DESIGN ITEM DEVELOPMENT

The design of the EBP Classroom Checklist began with a review of the NPDC EBP briefs (2010) and the NAC National Standards Project Report (2009) and all supportive studies cited by each. Decisions on which EBP to include in the benchmark assessment were made as follows. In order to make sure the measurement could be completed effectively during a 15- to 20-minute observation, EBP selected for the tool were restricted to those that would be observable in the classroom environment regardless of the type of instructional strategy implemented. The focus of the tool would be on observable and/or tangible supports (e.g., visual supports) rather than specific instructional strategies (e.g., discrete trial training). Developing a foundation for instruction including structures such as visual supports, schedules, and work systems is critical to providing instruction to students with ASD (Mesibov, Shea, & Schopler, 2005). In order to maintain this as a benchmark assessment, we are not measuring the implementation of evidence-based instructional strategies, rather we are measuring the observable measurable supports that promote, allow, or sustain these EBP. Additionally, recognizing that formal observation of instruction should be at least 20-30 minutes (Zepeda, 2013) and we were targeting the 10-15 minutes recommended for an informal observation (Zepeda, 2013), including specific instructional practices did not meet the intent of this tool (i.e., using informal classroom visits to facilitate collaborative problem solving). Table 1 outlines the evidence-based practices selected for the observation tool.

Following the selection of EBP, individual items were created that used the team's field-based knowledge of common language (Bos, 1995) accessible to practitioners, administrators, and related service personnel.

Measuring content validity

The next step in the development process was to assess the content validity of the items. To do this, a content analysis design was utilized. A content analysis design provides an

Table 1. Summary of NPDC EBP (2010), corresponding NAC EBP (2009), and the EBP selected observation tool

National Professional Development Center EBP	National Autism Center EBP	Examples of Corresponding EBP COT Indicator(s)
Prompting	Antecedent Package; Modeling	Environmental (e.g., 4a, 6c), Instructional (e.g., 18, 19), Communication (e.g., 25, 26)
Antecedent-Based Intervention	Antecedent Package	Environmental (e.g., 2, 9, 12), Instructional (e.g., 15, 17, 21), Communication (e.g., 25, 26)
Time Delay (systematic instruction)	Antecedent Package	Environmental (e.g., 6c) Instructional (e.g., 18), Communication (e.g., 25)
Reinforcement	Behavioral Package	Environmental (e.g., 6c, 7), Instructional (e.g., 16, 19), Communication (e.g., 25, 26)
Task Analysis	Behavioral Package	Environmental (e.g., 6), Instructional (e.g., 14, 16), Communication (e.g., 25, 26)
Discrete Trial Training (systematic instruction)	Behavioral Package	Environmental (e.g., 6c), Instructional (e.g., 18, 20), Communication (e.g., 25)
Functional Communication Training	Behavioral Package	Environmental (e.g., 8, 10), Instructional (e.g., 18), Communication (e.g., 23, 25)
Response Interruption/Redirection	Behavioral Package	Environmental (e.g., 4b, 8), Instructional (e.g., 18), Communication (e.g., 24, 25, 26)
Differential Reinforcement	Behavioral Package	Environmental (e.g., 6, 8), Instructional (e.g., 16, 18), Communication (e.g., 25, 26)
Social Narratives	Story-based Intervention Package	Environmental (e.g., 4b, 12), Communication (e.g., 25, 26)
Video Modeling	Modeling	Environmental (e.g., 6, 12), Instructional (e.g., 16, 19), Communication (e.g., 23, 25)
Naturalistic Interventions	Naturalistic Teaching Strategies	Environmental (e.g., 3, 11), Instructional (e.g., 16, 17, 19), Communication (e.g., 24, 27)
Peer-Mediated Intervention	Peer Training Package	Environmental (e.g., 2), Instructional (e.g., 13, 19), Communication (e.g., 25, 26, 27)
Pivotal Response Training	Pivotal Response Treatment	Instructional (e.g., 18)
Visual Supports	Schedules	Environmental (e.g., 1, 7), Instructional (e.g., 16, 17), Communication (e.g., 25, 26)
Structured Work Systems	Schedules	Environmental (e.g., 4b, 7, 12), Instructional (e.g., 15, 16), Communication (e.g., 25, 26)
Self-Management	Self-Management	Environmental (e.g., 4b, 6b), Instructional (e.g., 16, 18), Communication (e.g., 26)
Parent-Implemented Intervention		Not applicable
Social Skills Training Groups		Environmental (e.g., 1, 3, 4b), Instructional (e.g., 13, 19), Communication (e.g., 26)
Speech-Generating Devices		Environmental (e.g., 3, 4b), Instructional (e.g., 18, 19), Communication (e.g., 23, 24)
Computer Aided Instruction		Environmental (e.g., 4b), Instructional (e.g., 13, 19), Communication (e.g., 26)
Picture Exchange		Environmental (e.g., 9, 10), Instructional (e.g., 18), and Communication (e.g., 23, 25)
Communication System		Environmental (e.g., 4b, 10), Instructional (e.g., 18, 19), and Communication (all)
Extinction		Environmental (e.g., 4b, 8),

opportunity for experts in a particular field to assess the content of a tool or measure under development. This design provides a quantitative summary of the representativeness and clarity of each item as well as the expert panel's narrative suggestions for improving the measure (Rubio, Berg-Weger, Tebb, Lee, & Rauch, 2003).

Participants

To create a panel of experts for the content analysis, a minimum of three content experts was necessary (Lynn, 1986; Rubio et al., 2003). A content expert is defined as a professional who has worked extensively with this content and has published in the field. Lay experts were also included on the panel to ensure the practicality of the tool. A lay expert is defined as the people for whom the work is most critical in their day-to-day practice. Ten content experts and ten lay experts were solicited for participation as the expert panel to attempt to create a sample size of twenty that could provide comprehensive information about the measure (Rubio et al., 2003).

Recruitment Participants were recruited via email. The email outlined the purpose of the study and asked for their participation. It also included directions for completing and returning the scoring form that was sent with the email. As incentive for participation in the study, the email also explained that they would receive a copy of the tool in appreciation of their feedback.

Data collection

A content validity scale titled the Reviewer Response Form was developed. This scale required reviewers to score the items for representativeness (e.g., whether the item addresses EBP for students with autism and other significant disabilities) and clarity (whether the item listed was clear to the reader and observable). Representativeness was rated in one of four ways: (a) not representative, (b) requires major revisions to be representative, (c) requires some revision to be representative, and (d) representative. Reviewers also rated the clarity of each item on a similar scale: (a) not clear, (b) requires major revisions to be clear, (c) requires some revision to be clear, and (d) clear. The experts were also given space to make suggestions to improve the item.

In addition to representativeness and clarity, the Reviewer Response Form asked each reviewer to relate each item to a specific factor (physical organization, visual schedules, structured work systems, embedded instructional supports, visual supports, or other). Finally, each reviewer was asked to respond to open-ended questions related to the comprehensiveness of all of the items as a whole. Panelists were asked to specify their recommendations for adding or deleting any item.

Prior to administration with the expert panel, the Reviewer Response Form was piloted with two doctoral students with experience working with students with ASD. Feedback from the two pilot reviewers provided important information about the items in the rating scale and the content analysis design administration process. Pilot reviewers recommended more explicit directions related to completing and returning the instrument. Randomization of the Reviewer Response Form was identified as necessary for later factorial validity indices along with the addition of space for reviewers to include their demographic information. The form was updated and was distributed to the 20 panelists via email.

The expert panel was given explicit directions for completing and returning the Reviewer Response Form, as well as a suggested time frame for submission. Of the ten content experts and ten lay experts contacted, three content experts (two nationally recognized professors and one state-level consultant) and three lay experts (one teacher, one special education administrator, and one principal) returned the reviewer response form, meeting the minimum guidelines for response rates for a content analysis design as described by Rubio and colleagues (2003). These data were manually transferred from the Word document to the Excel data file created for data analysis.

A coding structure was created to represent the demographic information and questionnaire responses provided by the reviewers. Two individuals entered the data into the file (one read the data while the other typed). Once the data file was complete, the individuals switched roles to check for accuracy (one read the data while the other checked the entries). For the content validity design, data was entered sequentially by section (i.e., representativeness, clarity, factor) to create clarity in the process. To check for transcription errors, every 10th data entry was checked for each of the 6 reviewers. No entry errors were found in this process.

Data analysis

Overall, six panelists returned the Reviewer Response Form. Inter-rater agreement for representativeness of each item was determined by calculating the agreement among the experts. Rubio and colleagues (2003) recommend dichotomizing the scale for inter-rater agreement (e.g., either representative [3, 4] or not representative [1,2]) for both representativeness and clarity. Agreement for each item is determined by determining the number of experts rating the item representative or clear ($3\text{-}4n$) and dividing that number by the total number of experts (N). The number of items with a reliability score of at least .80 was divided by the total number of items on the scale in order to determine the expert reviewer reliability for the scale. This procedure is recommended for studies with a sample of experts that exceeds five (Lynn, 1986).

Additionally, the content validity index (CVI) of the tool was calculated to determine the extent to which each item and the overall tool represented EBP for students with autism (Rubio et al., 2003). The CVI for each individual item was calculated by dividing the number of experts rating 3 or 4 on representativeness on the item by the number of experts ($3\text{-}4n/N$). The CVI of the measure was then estimated by calculating the average CVI across the measure.

Finally, the tool was analyzed for its factorial validity index (FVI). To calculate the FVI for each item, the number of experts who correctly associated the item with the factor is divided by the total number of experts ($n+/N$). The average is taken across items to determine the FVI for the entire instrument.

Results

The results of all reliability measures during the content analysis phase are as follows. In representativeness, 44 of the 46 items had an IRA for representativeness of .80 or higher. Thus, the overall expert IRA for the representativeness of the tool was .96. In clarity, 40 of the 46 items had an IRA for clarity of .80 or higher making the overall IRA for clarity at .87. In content validity, all but two of the items were rated above the .80 criterion and the overall CVI for the observation tool was .95. In factorial validity, the overall FVI for the

Table 2. Examples from revision process

	Version 1 (reviewer response form)	Item Version 2 (pilot testing for implementation)	Item Version 3 (implementation and evaluation)
Item	All students have an individualized work system (IWS) for independent work tasks	Individualized work systems (IWS) are used for independent work tasks in order to communicate answers to four questions: What work? How much work? How do I know when I'm finished? What do I do next?	Individualized work systems (IWS) are used for independent work tasks in order to communicate answers to four questions: What work? How much work? How do I know when I'm finished? What do I do next? Check ✓ if IWS are observed in classroom but are not applicable to observed instruction (i.e., independent work activities not observed)
Rating Scale	n/a	1: Not Observed 2: Partial Implementation 3: Full Implementation	N/A Not Applicable *The practice or support is not applicable to the classroom and/or observation period. A score of "NO" (not observed) should be given if the structure or support should be observed and is not.* N/O Not Observed *The practice or support is not in place in the classroom. There is no observable evidence that the structure or support is used or is an emerging practice in the classroom.* E/P Emerging Practice *The practice or support is observable in the classroom but is still emerging, is used inconsistently, or implementation is not proficient.* P/I Proficient Implementation *The practice or support is observable in the classroom and is implemented with proficiency.*

measure was .88. Modifications Based on Content Analysis The results of the content analysis design meet the minimum levels of acceptability for IRA (.80), CVI (.80) and FVI (.80) as determined by Rubio and colleagues (2003). Representativeness (IRA = .96) and content validity (CVI = .95) were the strongest areas of the observation tool, indicating the experts felt that the items on the measure were representative of evidence-based structures and supports for students with autism.

A review of the items with the lowest inter-rater agreement indicated the items that were very specific to the field of autism (e.g., structured work systems) had the lowest ratings for clarity. Those items were revised in response to the inter-rater agreement issues and to reflect some of the narrative responses from reviewers. Two items in embedded instructional supports were substantially revised as well. See Table 2 for an exemplar of the item revision process throughout the project.

The Factorial Validity Index met the criteria of .80 of acceptability with a FVI of .88. Although this was acceptable, there were some areas that required revision. Analysis of individual items indicated that there might have been some confusion with the categories of factors provided, rather than with the items themselves. It was determined from these results and from narrative responses that fewer, broader categories might provide more clarity.

In addition to the revision of items, format was modified as well. Based on panelist feedback, the items were organized into three broad categories with subheadings. The layout was adjusted until all of the information required was included on one page. The rating scale for the observations was included at the top of the document. In addition, a user's guide was created as a companion document to provide further clarity regarding the tool. This guide included definitions of items as well as exemplars. The updated version of the tool was then determined ready for a pilot implementation study in a classroom environment.

PHASE 2: IMPLEMENTATION AND MODIFICATION

Initial Implementation Pilot Testing

Participants A purposive sample (Oliver, 2006) of three raters completed the observation tool in a brief observation of eight classrooms. Three raters were selected as the number threshold that would provide diverse perspectives in the observation without causing undue disruption in the classroom environment. The first rater was the instrument developer; the second was a doctoral student who was selected based on her experience with teaching students with ASD and with observing evidence-based practices in the classroom; and the third was the school district's autism classroom consultant who regularly observed in students with autism in a variety of classroom environments. Neither the doctoral student nor the autism consultant had any prior knowledge of the tool. The classrooms observed during the pilot were selected based on the following criteria: (a) at least one student with ASD received instruction in the classroom and (b) the classroom teacher was willing to have observers in the room. The three raters observed together two general education classrooms (one kindergarten, one high school science) and eight classrooms for students with multiple disabilities (four elementary, three middle school, and one high school).

Data Collection and Analysis All of the data in this phase of the study were collected on the same day. The instrument developer met with the other two raters at the site of the first classroom observations. They reviewed the observation tool and the procedures in the user guide for twenty minutes. The raters then entered the classroom and remained there for 12 minutes (c.f. Zepeda, 2013). The instrument developer kept time and indicated when it was time to leave the room. The raters were permitted to move around the classroom unless the classroom teacher indicated that the raters should remain in a certain area. In 6 of 8 classrooms, raters were allowed to move around. This procedure was followed in each of the eight classrooms. No discussion of scoring or observations occurred until after all eight observations were complete.

Results The inter-rater reliability for the raters was found to be Kappa = 0.501 ($p <. 0.001$), 95% CI (0.476, 0.526). An overall inter-rater reliability of .501 met criteria for moderate acceptability; however, statisticians typically prefer Kappa values to be at least .6 before claiming an instrument has a strong level of agreement (Landis & Koch, 1977). While the results of this phase of the pilot testing were very positive, the tool required further revision and pilot testing before it could be considered strongly reliable.

Each of the raters provided optional written feedback that led to other modifications. First, the raters indicated that while the user guide was a helpful reference in training, it was cumbersome to have to refer to a separate document for the rating scale. The scale on the observation tool was edited to include a rubric-style description of each of the ratings.

Second, items were revised to improve clarity and limit redundancy. Finally, the layout of the tool was adjusted to clarify where raters were to indicate their responses. After modifications, the tool was ready to be tested again.

Second Implementation Pilot Testing

Participants The second iteration of the pilot study used the same basic design as the first, but involved three different raters. The instrument developer was one of the raters in this study. The second rater was the supervisor of the classrooms and had previously worked as a speech-language pathologist for students with autism. The third rater was an autism consultant and former classroom teacher. In this iteration only four different classroom environments were available to study and all four were exclusive to students with ASD.

Data Collection and Analysis The observation protocol was nearly identical in each version of the pilot, although one notable change was made in the second in an attempt to refine the observation process. The training process was lengthened from twenty minutes to one hour. In addition to reviewing the observation tool and user guide, the participants practiced rating particular situations, discussed the rationale for their decision, and finally determined a normed rating for each scenario.

Results Fleiss' kappa was again used to analyze the data from the study ($n=192$). The interrater reliability for the raters was found to be Kappa = 0.684 ($p < 0.001$), 95% CI (0.550, 0.640). This overall interrater reliability met the standard for substantial agreement and exceeded the acceptability level of .6 that statisticians typically require before an instrument is determined to have a strong level of agreement (Landis & Koch, 1977).

Implications of Pilot Testing

Results of the pilot testing reveal positive indications for the reliability of the instrument. Both the first and second versions of the pilot testing had at least acceptable inter-rater reliability results (at .501 and .684). The second iteration of the pilot testing met additional level of rigor by exceeding the .6 level that many statisticians typically prefer (Landis & Koch, 1977). It is promising to note that the level of acceptability increased from the first pilot test to the second. The differences in the classroom demographics of the two iterations of the study indicated that the reliability differences between the two may correspond to the nature of the classroom environment, which was an important consideration for subsequent reliability testing. The second iteration of the pilot also indicated that a more comprehensive training process may have a positive impact on reliability. This training process provided important opportunities for raters practicing responses and developing norms. In response, revisions to the training process will include standardizing this practice by including video models that include guidance and rationales about scoring. The pilot tests also revealed that another expert review of the checklist would be beneficial both to the revision process and to solicit feedback about appropriate protocols for implementation, including systematic observer training.

PHASE 3: IMPLEMENTATION AND EVALUATION

To complete a larger implementation and evaluation of the tool, a research partnership was developed with a statewide center that facilitated the use of EBP for students with

ASD. This project included five facilitators with master's degrees in special education as well as one faculty member with an area of expertise in autism and other developmental disabilities.

The project director and staff met with the initial research team to discuss items on the instrument, clarity of the tool, and to review the user's guide. The project director and staff then correlated the benchmark assessment to their larger, comprehensive tool so that they could use them seamlessly in the classrooms in which they worked. After this training, the tool was updated to reflect clarity issues (e.g., include options for acknowledging supports visible in the classroom that are not part of the instructional activities during the observation) and the rating scale itself. The rating scale was physically shifted from the top to the bottom of the page, the likert-style numbers changed to representative acronyms (e.g., EP for emerging practice), and a brief description of the guidelines for each score was included on the tool. Table 2 provides an item revision exemplar and more detailed information about the changes to the rating scale.

Each facilitator delivered up to 6 checklists in 6 schools within a two-week period and provided feedback about the ease of use, clarity of use, and overall benefits/concerns in using the checklist. Because facilitators were in different parts of the state, reliability measures were not taken as paired observations were not possible. In total 22 checklists were administered (8 elementary schools, 7 middle schools, and 7 high schools). Overwhelmingly, facilitators reported the tool as valuable, easy to use, and meaningful for use in follow-up conversations with administrators and practitioners. Specific comments suggested the EBP CC was quick (i.e., able to complete it in a short amount of time once familiar with the instrument) and helpful in classroom observation (i.e., provided specific things to look for). Comments also suggested the EBP CC seemed more useful for elementary and self-contained classroom than high school general education classrooms, and some items such as "individualized work system" may need more explanation. Comments also indicated the scoring system needed revision (i.e., "P/I and E/P are more difficult to remember and longer to write than one letter, check or other mark. Probably minor issue, but I kept having to look at the scale.")

After these modifications, the tool was presented to 54 k-12 principals at a statewide principal's leadership conference. After reviewing the document, administrators were asked if they would consider the tool useful or not useful for their practice. Of the 38 tools received back, 92% (35) were marked "yes, I have a need for this tool in school/district." Additionally, principals were asked to provide information on items that were not understood or not observable. Responses yielded five items that needed additional clarification (item #5, 9, 16, 28, 23). Two items were included as non-observable (#5, 25). Principals made suggestions for additional items they would like to measure. Of the 38 responses returned, 92% said the measuring scale was clear but, even though it was marked as clear, several comments were made on this item. Table 3 details these comments.

Overwhelmingly principals indicated the need for such a tool in schools. As we hypothesized earlier, clarity and efficiency are highly prized components of any measurement tool for use by school personnel. To be useful in practice, benchmark measurements must be functional for those consumers for which they are intended. The tool is currently undergoing modifications based on the principals' feedback as well as the new iteration of the NPDC-ASD 2014 report (Wong et al., 2014). An IRB is underway to engage in additional testing with administrators, other school leaders, general educators, and special educators.

Table 3. Principal comments

Comments regarding additional items to include: display students work; add a technology part/ computers; if there is an inclusion teacher, is team/co-teaching taking place or is the sped teacher serving as an aide; evidence/ reinforcement—a growth versus fixed mindset of intelligence and learning

Comments regarding scale included: When do you use n/a? Under the measuring scale, it talks about Not observed (NO) clear but too wordy—needs simplification, should E/P and P/I be quantified? For example, is used inconsistently 50–70% of available opportunities. These are random percentages but might make it easier for the observer to have a line of demarcation among the 3 categories.

Other comments: This tool is time consuming. Administrators have so many tasks that we need something that can be done quickly as a 5- to 10-minute walk through; could form be on a spreadsheet so that multiple observations by multiple observers could be combined in order to more easily collect data over time and/or across learning environments?

DISCUSSION

Using EBP, educators must ensure that students with ASD, like all learners, are making progress in the general education curriculum (Simpson et al., 2011). However, teachers identify a variety of barriers to implementing EBP including access, confidence, and time (Williams & Coles, 2007). The purpose of this study was to describe the development of a standardized benchmark assessment, the EBP Classroom Checklist for Educators, designed to address these teacher-identified challenges.

The EBP CC details foundational practices in practitioner-friendly terms, providing what Bos (1995) describes as common language for school administrators/leaders, and general and special educators. Student directed benchmark tools serve a variety of purposes in schools. Similarly, the EBP CC will likely be used in a variety of ways and for differing purposes. Our goal for the EBP CC is to offer a collaborative benchmark tool that leads to increased use of evidence-based practices for students with ASD.

To this end, the study had three specific aims. These were to establish the content validity of the EBP CC, establish reliability of the benchmark assessment tool when used in a classroom environment by multiple raters, and explore user satisfaction.

The content validity measures suggest the items on the EBP CC are representative of the practices expected in serving students with ASD. Similarly, reliability measures suggest multiple raters can use the checklist with similar results, and in an efficient amount of time. Generally speaking, individuals who administered the EBP CC valued the tool, indicating it met a need in their schools. These same individuals also provided constructive feedback, suggesting the scoring guide needed to be tweaked.

Limitations

Several limitations were noted in the development of the EBP CC. Initially, three content and three lay experts provided feedback. While this meets the minimum requirements (Lynn, 1986; Rubio et al., 2003) additional content experts might have added to or changed the number of items, their representativeness and clarity. Another limitation relates to the level of knowledge by raters in Phase 2. Given that the raters had knowledge of autism and experience with EBP, broader piloting by less experienced teachers and school administrators might have proved beneficial. Additionally, rating a larger set of more diverse classrooms might have better informed modifications. In Phase 3, reliability measures would have improved the findings on the strength of the instrument. Procedural fidelity measures are needed on the training and implementation of the tool.

Implications for Research and Practice

Klingner and colleagues (2013) suggested, "researchers must strategically and systematically scale up implementation of EBPS in collaboration with district partners" (p. 195). However, before moving the checklist back into schools, a critical next research step is to revise the content of the checklist to align with the 2014 EBP report by Wong and colleagues. Upon revision, additional content validity analysis will be needed. Once the content is determined valid, research is needed to standardize implementation in schools.

At the building and classroom levels, administrators, school leaders, or classroom teachers could initiate using the EBP CC. For example, general or special education classroom teachers could use the tool proactively to self-assess and reflect on their existing practices as benchmarks throughout the school year. Teams of general and special educators could also use the EBP CC to guide collaborative assessment and planning. Future research is needed to investigate a variety of questions related to teacher implementation. For example, researchers might study teachers' ability to use the checklist independently or with very limited support, how the tool influences teacher reflection, and the influence of the EBP CC on teachers' feelings of efficacy. Researchers should also address the link between the tool and student progress; for example, do students in classrooms where teachers have systematically implemented the items on the checklist make greater progress than those who don't?

Beginning special educators, especially those servicing students with ASD and other complex learning needs, are faced with a variety of challenges. Some of these include building collaborative relationships with colleagues, addressing behavior needs of students, and organizing materials and data collection (Israel, Carnahan, Snyder, & Williamson, 2013). The EBP CC could be a powerful tool for these teachers, allowing them to systematically implement EBPs that are the foundation for student success. Future research should address the effectiveness of the EBP CC in systematically guiding beginning teachers in creating classroom systems for students with ASD. For example, researchers might evaluate effectiveness when a teacher moves through the checklist one component at a time versus a teacher who attempts to implement several practices at the same time.

Additionally, administrators and other school leaders could use the EBP CC as a reference tool during brief classroom visits. While this has been indicated as a desired use by administrators, perhaps a more important or valuable application would be to use the EBP CC as the foundation for collaborative problem solving and goal-setting between teachers and administrators or other school leaders. Research is needed to evaluate the effectiveness of the EBP CC in facilitating such collaboration. Additionally, researchers should address the capacity of these collaborative problem-solving efforts in highlighting specific evidence-based practices needed. Based on these specific needs, educators and/or administrators/leaders could access NPDC EBP briefs or NAC National Standards Project for more comprehensive references and supports, and/or plan building- or district-level professional development related to these practices. Similarly, the EBP CC could be used in districts or buildings to highlight the need for more extensive assessment and planning using comprehensive tools such as the LAQI (Lowrey et al., 2010) or the Tier 1 Classroom Checklist-ASD Nest Program (Bleiweiss, Hough, & Cohen, 2013).

Kucharczyk and colleagues (2012) described coaching as an important strategy for increasing the use of EBP. Several models have emerged (Israel et al., 2013; Kucharczyk et al., 2012) for coaching teachers of students with ASD and other significant disabilities. The EBP CC could serve as a model for guiding coaching observations and collaborative planning. Future research is needed to investigate the usefulness of the tool within these models. Specifically, research might consider the differences between the coaching outcomes when a specific tool such as the EBP CC is used. For example, researchers could evaluate the usefulness of the EBP CC in guide coach observations, facilitating coach-teacher discussions, or even in setting collaborative goals for teachers and coaches. Researchers might also investigate the EBP CC as a tool for sustaining progress upon completion of coaching, which can often be a challenge (Israel et al., 2013).

Finally, in addition to the school or district level use, the EBP CC could be used to help pre-service educators (administrators and teachers) examine the foundational EBP necessary for teaching students with ASD and other similar needs, a critical first step in improving education for students with ASD. For example, in their initial classroom observations, pre-service teachers could use the EBP CC to identify practices. These observations could serve as the foundation for reflection on the role of EBP. Research should address the effectiveness of the EBP CC on several levels in pre-service education. For example, researchers could investigate if the EBP CC supports pre-service educators in moving from low levels of understanding (e.g., identification of a specific practice) to higher levels (e.g., analysis and application)? Of equal importance would be to investigate the level of support or contextual factors necessary to encourage beginning special educators who used the EBP CC during their teacher training to use the tool as a foundation for practice in their first years.

CONCLUSION COMMENTS

School administrators and district leaders have consistently indicated a need for a tool such as the EBP CC, and educators have suggested such tools must be effective and efficient. The purpose of this study was to evaluate the content validity and reliability of the EBP CC. While additional research is needed, initial testing suggests the EBP CC is a feasible tool for establishing the foundational practices necessary for promoting positive outcomes for students with ASD.

REFERENCES

Billingsley, B. (2010). Work contexts matter: Practical considerations for improving new special educators' experiences in schools. Journal of Special Education Leadership, 23(1), 41–49.

Bleiweiss, J. D., Hough, L., & Cohen, S. (2013). Everyday Classroom Strategies and Practices for Supporting Children With Autism Spectrum Disorders. Shawnee Mission, KS: AAPC Publishing.

Bos, C. (1995). Professional development and teacher change: Encouraging news from the trenches. Remedial and Special Education, 16, 379-382. doi:10.1177/074193259501600610

Burns, M. K., & Ysseldyke, J. E. (2009). Reported prevalence of evidence-based instructional practices in special education. The Journal of Special Education, 43, 3–11.

California Department of Education Publication. "Common Benchmark Assessments" Retrieved 2014, March 26 from Taking Center Stage -- Act II: A Portal for Middle Grades Educators. Website: http://pubs.cde.ca.gov/TCSII/ch2/comnbnchmrkassess.aspx

Cook, B. & Odom, S. (2013). Evidence-based practices and implementation science in special education. Exceptional Children, 79, 135–144.

Cook, B., & Schirmer, B. (2003). What is special about special education? Overview and analysis. The Journal of Special Education, 37, 200–205. doi:10.1177/00224669030370031001

Cook, B. G., Tankersley, M., & Landrum, T. J. (2009). Determining evidence-based practices in special education. Exceptional Children, 75, 365–383.

Domitrovich, C. E., Bradshaw, C. P., Poduska, J. M., Hoagwood, K., Buckley, J. A., ... Ialongo, N. S. (2008). Maximizing the implementation quality of evidence-based preventive interventions in schools: a conceptual framework. Advances in School Mental Health Promotion, 1, 6-28. Doi. 10.1080/1754730X.2008.9715730

Herman, J. L., Osmundson, E., & Dietel, R. (2010). Benchmark assessments for improved learning (AACC Policy Brief). Los Angeles, CA: University of California. Individuals with Disabilities Education Improvement Act of 2004, Pub. L. 108-446, 118 (2004).

Israel, M., Carnahan, C., *Snyder, K. & Williamson, P. (2013). Supporting new teachers of students with significant disabilities through virtual coaching: A proposed model. Remedial and Special Education, 34, 195–204. doi. 10.1177/0741932512450517.

Jones, M. L. (2009). A study of novice special educators' views of evidence-based practices. Teacher Education and Special Education, 32, 101-120. doi. 10.1177/0888406409333777

Klingner, J. K., Boardman, A. G., & McMaster, K. L. (2013). What does it take to scale up and sustain evidence based practices? Exceptional Children, 79, 195–211.

Klingner, J. K., Boardman, A. G., & McMaster, K. L. (2013). What does it take to scale up and sustain evidence-based practices?. *Exceptional Children, 79*(2), 195–211.

Kucharczyk, S., Shaw, E., Smith Myles, B., Sullivan, L., Szidon, K., & Tuchman-Ginsberg, L. (2012). Guidance & coaching on evidence based practices for learners with autism spectrum disorders. Chapel Hill: The University of North Carolina, Frank Porter Graham Child Development Institute, National Professional Development Center on Autism Spectrum Disorders.

Landis, J. R., & Koch, G. G. (1977). The measurement of observer agreement for categorical data. biometrics, 33, 159–174. doi. 10.2307/2529310

Lowrey, K. A., Wilson, P., Altman, L., Riley, J., Hammons, D., Polotzola, B., & Blanco, M. (2010). Guide to Louisiana Autism Quality Indicators for Schools. New Orleans, LA: Louisiana Autism Spectrum and Related Disabilities Project, Human Development Center, Louisiana State University Health Sciences Center. Retrieved from: http://www.hdc.lsuhsc.edu/lasard/pdf/UsersGuide2010 FINAL.pdf

Lynn, M. R. (1986). Determination and quantification of content validity. Nursing Research, 35, 382–385.

McLeskey, J. & Billingsley, B. S. (2008). How does the quality and stability of the teaching force influence the research-to-practice gap? A perspective on the teacher shortage in special education. Remedial and Special Education, 29, 293-305. Doi. 10.1177/0741932507312010

Mesibov, G., Shea, V., & Schopler, E. (2005). The TEACCH approach to autism spectrum disorders. New York: Kluwer Academic/Plenum.

National Autism Center. (NAC). (2009). National standards report: Addressing the need for evidence-based practice guidelines for autism spectrum disorders. Randolph, MA: author. No Child Left Behind Act of 2001, 20 U.S.C. S. 4114. (2001).

National Professional Development Center on Autism Spectrum Disorders. (NPDC on ASD). (nd). Evidence based practice briefs. Retrieved from http://autismpdc.fpg.unc.edu/content/briefs

Odom, S. L., Boyd, B. A., Hall, L. J., & Hume, K. (2010). Evaluation of comprehensive treatment models for individuals with autism spectrum disorders. Journal of Autism and Developmental Disorders, 40, 425–436. doi. 10.1007/s10803-009-0825-1

Odom, S. L., Cox, A. W., & Brock, M. E. (2013). Implementation science, professional development, and autism spectrum disorders. Council for Exceptional Children, 79, 233-251.

Odom, S. L., Duda, M. A., Cox, A. W., & Stabel, A. (2014). Implying an implementation science framework for adoption of a comprehensive program for high school students with autism spectrum disorder. Hammill Institute on Disabilities, 35, 123-132.

Oliver, P. (2006) Purposive Sampling, in Jupp, V. (ed). The Sage dictionary of social research methods. Sage.

Olson, L. (2005a). Benchmark assessments offer regular checkups on student achievement. Education Week, 25, 13-14.

Olson, L. (2005b). State test programs mushroom as NCLB mandate kicks in. Education Week, 20, 10-14.

Rohrbach, L. A., Grana R., Sussman, S., & Valente, T. W. (2006). Type II translation: Transporting prevention interventions from research to real world settings. Evaluation & the Health Professions, 29, 302-333. doi. 10.1177/0163278706290408

Rubio, D., Berg-Weger, M., Tebb, S. S., Lee, E. S., & Rauch, S. (2003). Objectifying content validity: Conducting a content validity study in social work research. Social Work Research, 27, 94-104. doi: 10.1093/swr/27.2.94

Simpson, R. L. (2004). Finding effective intervention and personal preparation practices for students with autism spectrum disorders. Exceptional Children, 70, 135-144. doi. 10.1177/001440290407000201

Simpson, R. L. (2005). Evidence based practices and students with autism spectrum disorders. Focus on Autism and Other Developmental Disabilities, 20, 140-149. Doi. 10.1177/10883576050200030201

Simpson, R., Mundschenk, N., and Heflin, J. (2011). Issues, policies, and recommendations for improving the education of learners with autism spectrum disorders. Journal of Disability Policy Studies (22), 3-17. doi. 10.1177/1044207310394850

Williams, D., & Coles, L. (2007). Teachers' approaches to finding and using research evidence: an information literacy perspective. Educational research, 49, 185-206. doi. 10.1080/00131880701369719

Wong, C., Odom, S., Hume, K., Cox., A., Fettig, A., Kucharczyk., S., . . . Schultz., T. (2014). Evidence-based practices for children, youth, and young adults with Autism Spectrum Disorder. Chapel Hill: The University of North Carolina, Frank Porter Graham Child Development Institute, Autism Evidence-Based Practice Review Group.

Zepeda, S. J. (2013). The principal as instructional leader: A handbook for supervisors. Routledge.

Correspondence concerning this article should be addressed to Christina R. Carnahan, University of Cincinnati, College of Education, School of Education, Special Education, PO Box 210022, Cincinnati, OH 45221. E-mail: Christi.carnahan@uc.edu

Glossary

AAC *See* augmentative and alternative communication.

ABA *See* applied behavior analysis.

action-oriented strategies Strategies that employ practical action to achieve goals.

Americans with Disabilities Act (ADA) of 1990 Guarantees that individuals with disabilities have equal opportunities in employment, public accommodation, transportation, government services, both state and local, and telecommunications. ADA also provides individuals with disabilities the same civil rights protection provided to all individuals based on race, sex, national origin, or religion.

applied behavior analysis (ABA) Based on the principles of learning theory, the process of applying interventions systematically to improve socially significant behavior to a meaningful degree.

ASD *See* autism spectrum disorder.

attending skills Basic attention skills required to provide one's focus on another individual.

augmentative and alternative communication (AAC) system Refers to any technology that allows for communication other than natural speech, including sign language, picture exchange, or speech-generating devices.

autism spectrum disorder (ASD) An umbrella term for a group of disorders characterized by difficulties with social interaction and communication as well as repetitive behaviors.

best or recommended practices Practices that are often promoted but have no agreed-on criteria to support their use.

case law Provides clarity relevant to current legislation and regulations based on previous court decisions. These court cases will be similar in nature to the current legislation and regulations.

CEC *See* Council for Exceptional Children.

central coherence Refers to the ability to focus on the important information in a situation and then use the information appropriately. Individuals with ASD may find it difficult to identify the big picture from information given or situations encountered, which may lead to a theory of weak central coherence.

Child Find Mandated under IDEA as the referral process to ensure all students in need receive the support provided through special education services. Once referred, an evaluation will be required before services are provided.

collaboration Working together to create results. This could involve collaboration among school leaders, general education teachers, special education teachers, school psychologists, specialized professionals, consultants, paraprofessionals, and parents to produce optimal results for the student's success.

Council for Exceptional Children (CEC) A professional organization of educators working together to ensure the best outcomes for children with special needs.

developmental delay A delay in the mental or physical development of a child.

discrete trial training Procedure used in ABA that breaks down skills into smaller components to increase successful responding. Correct responses are positively reinforced to increase the likelihood of skill acquisition.

distributed leadership School leadership model that promotes staff participation in the school's decision-making processes and encourages leadership roles of teachers with more experience or knowledge of a specific practice to mentor other colleagues.

due process hearing Requested through a due process complaint relating to a child with a disability and the identification, evaluation, or education placement of the child regarding FAPE.

EF *See* executive function.

efficacy The capacity to produce the targeted outcome or results.

ESY *See* extended school year services.

Every Student Succeeds Act (ESSA) of 2015 The act formerly referred to as the No Child Left Behind Act of 2001 and originating from the Elementary and Secondary Act of 1965.

evidenced-based practices Interventions that demonstrate efficacy and meet specific criteria of reliability and validity.

executive function (EF) Individuals with ASD often struggle with EFs, such as complex planning, reasoning, or organizing, which could present itself in difficulties completing multistep tasks or planning for future activities.

extended school year (ESY) services Mandated under IDEA for qualifying students with disabilities to maintain progress by providing individualized services during breaks from school.

fidelity The extent to which an intervention was performed as intended.

free appropriate public education (FAPE) Mandated under IDEA through an IEP, special education or related services provided by public preschools, elementary schools, or secondary schools to meet the standards of the state education agency.

graphic organizer Tool that uses visual representations of information to supplement textual or instructional learning.

IDEA *See* Individuals with Disabilities Education Act.

IEP *See* individualized education program.

implementation drivers Processes that can be maximized to increase the successful implementation of evidence-based practices. Competency, organization, and leadership are the three categories of implementation drivers.

improvement science Science of asking questions to determine problems with implementation.

independent educational evaluation A private evaluation outside of the school system's evaluation.

individualized education program (IEP) Document created for each individual student receiving special education or services to meet his or her specific needs.

Individuals with Disabilities Education Act (IDEA) of 1990 Federal law requiring states and public agencies to provide services to individuals with disabilities from birth to the age of 21.

innovation science Science of using innovation, such as evidence-based practices, in the school setting.

joint attention Also called *shared attention*. It refers to drawing another person's interest toward an object or activity and checking that the person is sharing attention to that object or activity. Deficit in joint attention is one of the characteristics of ASD.

least restrictive environment (LRE) Implemented under IDEA as the opportunity for students with disabilities to be educated to the greatest extent possible with students without disabilities.

legislation Laws established by the state or federal government.

LRE *See* least restrictive environment.

major life activity Any function that is important to an individual's daily life, including breathing, caring for one's self, hearing, performing manual tasks, seeing, sleeping, talking, walking, or working.

mediation A trained mediator will be provided by the school district to impartially attempt to mediate a resolution between the parties.

naturalistic interventions Strategies based on principles of ABA that build on a child's naturally occurring exchanges and activities.

other health impaired Mandated under IDEA as an individual with limited strength, vitality, or alertness as well as heightened alertness in the educational setting negatively affecting performance.

pedagogical Related to the practice of teaching.

peer-reviewed research The evaluation of research by experts in the same field of study.

practice-based evidence Practitioners use of evidence-based practices.

priming An antecedent intervention that allows the student to preview activities or information in a low-demand scenario in preparation for upcoming participation or instruction.

prior written notice Parental consent obtained prior to conducting an evaluation as well as before initial placement into a special education program.

procedural errors Occur when federal requirements for developing an IEP are not followed by the school district personnel.

procedural safeguards Mandated under IDEA to provide parents equal participation in the special education process.

progress monitoring Using data throughout the implementation of an intervention to ensure effectiveness of an intervention or program.

promising practices Practices that have demonstrated effectiveness but need further investigation to meet the criteria for an evidenced-based practice.

reculturing Changing the culture of an organization to better align with its goals.

regression and recoupment Occurs when a student does not retain skills learned during long breaks from school as well as the time required to regain the previously learned skills.

regulation How the specific legislation will be implemented as well as enforced.

Rehabilitation Act of 1973 Civil rights law requiring equivalent education provided for students with and without disabilities.

reinforcement Consequences that follow a behavior that increase the likelihood of that behavior occurring in the future.

related services Mandated under IDEA through an IEP and provided by public preschools or elementary or secondary schools to meet the standards of the SEA not provided by special education, including developmental, corrective, or other supportive services to increase the benefit of special education.

research-based practices Another term for evidence-based practices.

school culture The beliefs and expectations in how a school operates.

scripted language Also called *echolalia*. It is common in individuals with ASD and refers to the repetition of words or sounds copied from another person's speech, the movies, a television show, songs, or books.

SEA *See* state educational agency.

Section 504 accommodation plan Provides appropriate educational support and services for students with disabilities that do not meet the IDEA eligibility requirements.

self-regulation An executive function that allows one to manage his or her own behavior. Individuals with ASD may have a deficit in self-regulation, which prevents them from monitoring and preventing maladaptive behavior.

social-communication Individuals with ASD have differences in social-communication from their typically developing peers in social-emotional reciprocity; nonverbal communication used for social interaction; and the development, maintenance, and understanding of relationships.

standards An agreed-on criteria to establish acceptability. Evidence-based practices require 1) two high-quality experimental or quasi-experimental group design studies; 2) five high-quality single-subject design studies conducted by three different researchers or research groups; 3) one high-quality randomized or quasi-experimental group design study and three high-quality single-subject design studies conducted by at least three different investigators or research groups (across the group and single-subject design studies).

STAR method A behavioral interview method that asks candidates to describe the situation, task, action, and results of how an interviewee handled a past experience.

state complaint resolution process Mandated under IDEA and directly controlled by the SEA for resolving disputes in a less costly and more efficient method than the due process hearing.

state educational agency (SEA) The government agency at the state level supervising public elementary and secondary schools. The SEA is known as the department of education or the state board of education in some states.

stereotyped movements Aimless and repetitive physical movements.

substantive errors Occur when an IEP fails to provide educational benefit because federal requirements for development are not followed.

task analysis Breaking a skill into its smallest components to teach each step of the skill and then chaining those steps together to perform a more complex task.

theory of mind (ToM) The hypothesis that individuals with ASD lack an awareness of the feelings of others. They do not understand that the plans, emotions, and points of view of others may differ from their own.

time delay Procedure used to fade the use of prompts necessary for responding. A delay is installed between the demand and the use of a prompt. Independent responding is positively reinforced to increase the likelihood of future independent responding.

ToM *See* theory of mind.

transition statements Anticipated postsecondary program with measurable goals as well as a description of individual services needed to meet goals.

video modeling A strategy in which an individual is taught a skill through observing a model of that skill on video.

visual schedule A visual representation of an individual's schedule that shows what tasks have been completed, what tasks are in progress, and what tasks come next.

visual supports Visual representations that increase comprehension, language, and expectations. Picture exchange cards, visual schedules, and TEACCH are examples of visual supports.

zero reject Implemented under IDEA as special education services provided for all students with disabilities, regardless of severity.

References

Able, H., Sreckovic, M. A., Schultz, T. R., Garwood, J. D., & Sherman, J. (2015). Views from the trenches: Teacher and student supports needed for full inclusion of students with ASD. *Teacher Education and Special Education, 38,* 44–57.

Adamson, L., Bakeman, R., & Deckner, D. (2004). The development of symbol infused joint attention. *Child Development, 75*(4), 1171–1187.

AK v. Alexandria City School, 484 F.3d 672 (4th Cir. 2007).

Alberto, P. A., & Troutman, A. C. (2009). *Applied behavioral analysis for teachers* (8th ed.). Upper Saddle River, NJ: Prentice Hall.

American Psychological Association. (2013). *Diagnostic and statistical manual of mental disorders* (5th ed.). Washington, DC: Author.

Americans with Disabilities Act (ADA) of 1990, PL 101-336, 42 U.S.C. §§ 12101 *et seq.*

Appellant v. Commonwealth of Pennsylvania, Department of Public Welfare (3d Cir. 2004).

Attwood, T. (2008). An overview of autism spectrum disorders. In K. D. Buron & P. Wolfberg (Eds.), *Learners on the autism spectrum: Preparing highly qualified educators* (pp. 18–43). Shawnee Mission; KS: Autism Asperger Publishing.

Banda, D. R., Grimmett, E., & Hart, S. L. (2009). Activity schedules: Helping students with autism spectrum disorders in general education classrooms manage transition issues. *Teaching Exceptional Children, 41*(4), 16–21.

Baron-Cohen, S., Leslie, A., & Frith, U. (1985). Does the autistic child have a "theory of mind?" *Cognition, 21,* 37–46.

Bass, J. (2014, April). *Building executive functioning and organizational skills in individuals with ASD.* Presentation at The Kelly O'Leary Center for Autism Spectrum Disorders, Division of Developmental and Behavioral Pediatrics, Cincinnati Children's Hospital Medical Center.

Bateman, B. D. (2011). Individual education programs for children with disabilities. In J. M. Kauffman & D. P. Hallahan (Eds.), *Handbook of special education* (pp. 77–90). Philadelphia, PA: Taylor & Francis/Routledge.

Bend Lapine Sch. Dist. v. K.H., IDELR 191 (D. Ore. 2005).

Beukelman, D.R., & Mirenda, P. (2013). *Augmentative and alternative communication: Supporting children and adults with complex communication needs* (4th ed.). Baltimore, MD: Paul H. Brookes Publishing Co.

Bishop, D., & Norbury C. F. (2005). Executive functions in children with communication impairments in relation to autistic symptomatology: 2: Response inhibition. *Autism, 9*(1), 29–43.

Boyd, B. A., Conroy, M. A., Mancil, G. R., Nakao, T., & Alter, P. J. (2007). Effects of circumscribed interests on the social behaviors of children with autism spectrum disorders. *Journal of Autism and Developmental Disorder, 37*(8), 1550–1561. doi: 10.1007/s10803-006-0286-8

Boyle, C. A., Boulet, S., Schieve, L. A., Cohen, R. A., Blumberg, S. J., Yeargin-Allsopp, M.,... Kogan, M. D. (2011). *Pediatrics, 127,* 1034–1042.

Bradshaw, C. P., Koth, C. W., Thornton, L. A., & Leaf, P. J. (2009). Altering school climate through school-wide positive behavioral interventions and supports: Findings from a group-randomized effectiveness trial. *Prevention science, 10,* 100–115.

Brady, N. C., Bruce, S., Goldman, A., Erickson, K., Mineo, B., Ogletree, B. T., ... Schoonover, J. (2016). Communication services and supports for individuals with severe disabilities: Guidance for assessment and intervention. *American Journal on Intellectual and Developmental Disabilities, 121*(2), 121–138.

Bryan, L. C., & Gast, D. L. (2000). Teaching on-task and on-schedule behaviors to high-functioning children with autism via picture activity schedules. *Journal of Autism and Developmental Disorders, 30*(6), 553–567. doi:10.1023/A:1005687310346

Bryk, A. S., Gomez, L. M., & Grunow, A. (2010), *Getting ideas into action: Building networked improvement communities in education.* Retrieved from https://www.carnegiefoundation.org/resources/publications/getting-ideas-action-building-networked-improvement-communities-education/

Bulgran, J., & Carta, J. (1993). Examining the instructional contexts of students with learning disabilities. *Exceptional Children, 59,* 182–191.

Bucks County Department of Mental Health/Mental Retardation v. Pennsylvania, 379 F.3d 61 (3d Cir. 2004).

Carnahan, C. (2006). Engaging children with autism and their teachers. *Teaching Exceptional Children, 39*(2), 44–50.

Carnahan, C., Hume, K., Clarke, L., & Borders, C. (2009). Using structured work systems to promote independence and engagement for students with autism spectrum disorders. *Teaching Exceptional Children, 41*(4), 6–14.

Carnahan, C., & Snyder, K. (2011). *Rules and routines: Online training module.* Columbus, OH: Ohio Center for Autism and Low Incidence.

Carnahan, C., & Williamson, P. (2010). Autism, cognition, and reading. In C. Carnahan & P. Williamson (Eds.), *Quality literacy instruction for students with autism spectrum disorders* (pp. 21–44). Shawnee Mission, KS: Autism Asperger Publishing.

Carnahan, C. R., & Williamson, P. (2016). Systematically teaching students with autism spectrum disorder about expository text structures. *Intervention in School and Clinic, 51*(5), 293–300.

Carnahan, C. R., Williamson, P., Clarke, L., & Sorensen, R. (2009). A systematic approach for supporting paraeducators in educational settings: A guide for teachers. *Teaching Exceptional Children, 41*(5), 34–43.

Carr, M. E., Moore, D. W., & Anderson, A. (2014). Self-management interventions on students with autism: A meta-analysis of single-subject research. *Exceptional Children, 81,* 28–44.

Carter, E. W., Cushing, L. S., Clark, N. M., & Kennedy, C. H. (2005). Effects of peer support interventions on students' access to the general curriculum and social interactions. *Research and Practice for Persons with Severe Disabilities, 30,* 15–25.

Carter, E. W., Common, E. A., Sreckovic, M. A., Huber, H. B., Bottema-Beutel, K., Gustafson, J. R., ... Hume, K. (2014). Promoting social competence and peer relationships for adolescents with autism spectrum disorders. *Remedial and Special Education, 35*(2), 91–101.

CAST. (2011). *Universal design for learning guidelines version 2.0.* Wakefield, MA: Author.

CAST. (2015). *What is UDL?* Retrieved from http://www.udlcenter.org/aboutudl/whatisudl

Cengher, M., Shamoun, K., Moss, P., Roll, D., Feliciano, G., & Fienup, D. M. (2016). A comparison of the effects of two prompt-fading strategies on skill acquisition in children with autism spectrum disorders. *Behavior Analysis in Practice, 9*(2), 115–125.

Chan, J., Lang, R., Rispoli, M., O'Reilly, M., Sigafoos, J., & Cole, H. (2009). Use of peer-mediated interventions in the treatment of autism spectrum disorders: A systematic review. *Research in Autism Spectrum Disorders, 3*(4), 876–889.

Christopher M. v. Corpus Christi Ind. School Dist., 933 F.2d 1285 (5th Cir. 1991).

Cihak, D. F. (2011). Comparing pictorial and video modeling activity schedules during transitions for students with autism spectrum disorders. *Research in Autism Spectrum Disorders, 5*(1), 433–441. doi:10.1016/j.rasd.2010.06.006

Cihak, D., Fahrenkrog, C., Ayres, K. M., & Smith, C. (2010). The use of video modeling via a video iPod and a system of least prompts to improve transitional behaviors for students with autism spectrum disorders in the general education classroom. *Journal of Positive Behavior Interventions, 12,* 103–115.

Civil Rights Act of 1964, PL 88-352, 20 U.S.C. §§ 241 *et seq.*

Coffin, A. B., & Bassity, K. (2007). *Home base: Online training module.* Columbus, OH: Ohio Center for Autism and Low Incidence.

Collins, B. C. (2012). *Systematic instruction for students with moderate and severe disabilities.* Baltimore, MD: Paul H. Brookes Publishing Co.

Conroy, T., Yell, M. L., Katsiyannis, A., & Collins, T. S. (2010). The U.S. Supreme Court and parental rights under the Individuals with Disabilities Education Act. *Focus on Exceptional Children, 43*(2), 1–14, 16.

Cook, B. G., & Cook, S. C. (2011). Thinking and communicating clearly about evidence-based practices in special education. *Arlington, VA: Council for Exceptional Children.*

Cook, B. G., & Cook, S. C. (2013). Unraveling evidence-based practices in special education. *Journal of Special Education, 47*(2), 71–82.

Cook, B. G., Tankersley, M., & Landrum, T. J. (Eds.). (2013). *Evidence-based practices* (Vol. 26). West Yorkshire, England: Emerald Group Publishing.

Corpus Christi Indep. Sch. Dist. v. Christopher N., 45 IDELR 221 (S.D. Tx. 2006).

Coucouvanis, J. (2005). *Super skills: A social skills program for children with Asperger syndrome, high functioning autism and related challenges.* Shawnees Mission, KS: Autism Asperger Publishing.

County School Bd. of Henrico County, Vir. v. RT, 433 F. Supp. 2d 692 (E.D. Va. 2006).

Darling-Hammond, L., LaPointe, M., Meyerson, D., Orr, M. T., & Cohen, C. (2007). *Preparing school leaders for a changing world: Lessons from exemplary leadership development programs.* Stanford, CA: Stanford Educational Leadership Institute.

Darrow, A. A. (2016). The Every Student Succeeds Act. *General Music Today, 30*(1), 41–44.

Dawson, G., Toth, K., Abbott, R., Osterling, J., Munson, J., Estes, A., & Liaw, J. (2004). Early social attention impairments in autism: Social orienting, joint attention, and attention to distress. *Developmental Psychology, 40*(2), 271–283.

Deal v. Hamilton County Bd. of Educ., 392 F.3d 840 (6th Cir. 2004).

Dean, C. B., Hubbell, E. R., Pitler, H., & Stone, B. J. (2012). *Classroom instruction that works: Research-based strategies for increasing student achievement.* Alexandria, VA: ASCD Publications.

DiStefano, C., Shih, W., Kaiser, A., Landa, R., & Kasari, C. (2016). Communication growth in minimally verbal children with ASD: The importance of interaction. *Autism Research, 9*(10), 1093–1102.

Dixon, M. R., & Cummings, A. (2001). Self-control in children with autism: Response allocation during delays to reinforcement. *Journal of Applied Behavior Analysis, 34*(4), 491–495.

Douglas, S. N., Chapin, S. E., & Nolan, J. F. (2016). Special education teachers' experiences supporting and supervising paraeducators: Implications for special and general education settings. *Teacher Education and Special Education, 39*(1), 60–74.

Dunlap, G., & Fox, L. (2002). *The challenge of autism from a large systems perspective.* Unpublished manuscript. University of South Florida, Tampa.

Dunlap, G., & Robbins, F. R. (1991). Current perspectives in service delivery for young children with autism. *Comprehensive Mental Health Care, 1,* 177–194.

Dunn-Buron, K. (2014, December). *When my worries get too big! Understanding emotional regulation and social stress as they impact explosive behavior.* Presentation at Xavier University, Cincinnati, Ohio.

Dymond, S. K., Renzaglia, A., Rosenstein, A., Chun, E. J., Banks, R. A., Niswander, V., & Gilson, C. L. (2006). Using a participatory action research approach to create a universally designed inclusive high school science course: A case study. *Research and Practice for Persons with Severe Disabilities, 31,* 293–308. doi:10.1177/154079690603100403

Education for All Handicapped Children Act of 1975, PL 94-142, 20 U.S.C. §§ 1400 *et seq.*

EG v. City School Dist. of New Rochelle, 606 F. Supp. 2d 384 (S.D.N.Y. 2009).

Elementary and Secondary Education Act of 1965, PL 89-10, 20 U.S.C. §§ 241 *et seq.*

Elliott, S. N., & Clifford, M. (2014). *Principal assessment: Leadership behaviors known to influence schools and the learning of all students* (Document No. LS-5). Retrieved from http://ceedar.education.ufl.edu/wp-content/uploads/2014/09/LS-5_FINAL_09-26-14.pdf

Emery, J., Applin, J. L., & Boman, M. (2013). A review of choice and preference assessments to increase academic attainment for autism spectrum disorders. *Kentucky Teacher Education Journal: The Journal of the Teacher Education Division of the Kentucky Council for Exceptional Children, 2*(1), 3.

Endrew F. v. Douglas County School District RE-1, 580 U.S. (2017).

Every Student Succeeds Act of 2015, PL 114-95, § 114 Stat. 1177.

Fettig, A. (2013a). *Functional communication training (FCT) fact sheet.* Chapel Hill, NC: University of North Carolina, Frank Porter Graham Child Development Institute, The National Professional Development Center on Autism Spectrum Disorders.

Fettig, A. (2013b). *Social skills training (SST) fact sheet.* Chapel Hill, NC: University of North Carolina, Frank Porter Graham Child Development Institute, The National Professional Development Center on Autism Spectrum Disorders.

Finnegan, E., & Accardo, A. L. (2017). Written expression in individuals with autism spectrum disorder: A meta-analysis. *Journal of autism and developmental disorders,* 1–15.

Finnegan, E., & Mazin, A. L. (2016). Strategies for increasing reading comprehension skills in students with autism spectrum disorder: A review of the literature. *Education and Treatment of Children, 39*(2), 187–219.

Fisher, N., & Happe, F. (2005). A training study of theory of the mind and executive function in children with autistic spectrum disorders. *Journal of Autism and Developmental Disorders, 35*(6), 757–771.

Fixsen, D., Blase, K., Naoom, S., & Duda, M. (2013–2015). *Implementation drivers: Assessing best practices.* Chapel Hill, NC: National Implementation Research Network.

Fixsen, D., Blase, K., Van Dyke, M., & Metz, A. (n.d.). *National implementation research network.* Retrieved from http://nirn.fpg.unc.edu

Fleury, V. P. (2013). *Discrete trial teaching (DTT) fact sheet.* Chapel Hill, NC: University of North Carolina, Frank Porter Graham Child Development Institute, The National Professional Development Center on Autism Spectrum Disorders.

Foxborough Reg. Charter Sch., 4 ECLPR 770, SEA MA, 2006.

Frith, U. (2003). *Autism: Explaining the enigma* (2nd ed.). Oxford, UK: Blackwell.

Frith, U. (2008). *How cognitive theories can help us explain autism.* Presentation at the U.C. Davis Mind Institute, Sacramento, CA.

Fullan, M. (1999). *Change forces: The sequel.* London, UK: Falmer.

Fullan, M. (2007). *The new meaning of educational change* (4th ed.). New York, NY: Teachers College Press.

Gersten, R., Woodward, J., & Darch, C. (1986). Direct instruction: A research-based approach to curriculum design and teaching. *Exceptional Children, 53,* 17–31.

Geurts, H., Verte, S., Oosterlaan, J., Roeyers, H., & Sergeant, J. (2004). How specific are executive function deficits in attention deficit hyperactivity disorder and autism? *Journal of Child Psychology and Psychiatry, 45*(4), 836–854.

Gresham, F. M., Beebe-Frankenberger, M., & MacMillan, D. L. (1999). A selective review of treatments for children with autism: Description and methodological considerations. *School Psychology Review, 28*(4), 559–575.

Hall, C., Hollingshead, A., & Christman, J. (2017). Implementing Video Modeling to Improve Transitions Within Activities in Inclusive Classrooms. *Intervention in School and Clinic,* doi.org/10.1177/1053451217736870.

Hall, L. J. (2015). Sustaining evidence-based practices by graduated special educators of students with ASD: Creating a community of practice. *Teacher Education and Special Education, 38,* 28–43.

Heflin, L., & Simpson, R. (1998). Interventions for children and youth with autism: Prudent choices in a world of exaggerated claims and empty promises. Part 1: Intervention and treatment option review. *Focus on Autism and Other Developmental Disabilities, 13*(4), 194–211.

Heifetz, R. A., Grashow, A., & Linsky, M. (2009). *The practice of adaptive leadership.* Boston, MA: Harvard Business Press.

Hendrix, R., Palmer, K., Tarshis, N., & Garcia-Winner, M. (2013) *The incredible flexible you.* San Jose, CA: Social Thinking Publishing.

Hill, E. (2004). Executive dysfunction in autism. *Trends in Cognitive Sciences, 8*(1), 26–32.

Hochman, J. M., Carter, E. W., Bottema-Beutel, K., Harvey, M. N., & Gustafson, J. R. (2015). Efficacy of peer networks to increase social connections among high school students with and without autism spectrum disorder. *Exceptional Children, 82*(1), 96–116.

Hoevemeyer, V. A. (2006). *High-impact interview questions: 701 behavior-based questions to find the right person for every job.* New York, NY: Amacom.

Hollocks, M. J., Jones, C. R., Pickles, A., Baird, G., Happé, F., Charman, T., & Simonoff, E. (2014). The association between social cognition and executive functioning and symptoms of anxiety and depression in adolescents with autism spectrum disorders. *Autism Research, 7*(2), 216–228.

Hoppey, D., & McLeskey, J. (2013). A case study of principal leadership in an effective inclusive school. *Journal of Special Education, 46,* 245–256.

Horner, R. H., & Sugai, G. (2015). School-wide PBIS: An example of applied behavior analysis implemented at a scale of social importance. *Behavior Analysis in Practice, 8*(1), 80–85.

Hume, K. (2008). *Overview of visual supports.* Chapel Hill, NC: University of North Carolina, Frank Porter Graham Child Development Institute, The National Professional Development Center on Autism Spectrum Disorders.

Hume, K. (2013). *Visual supports (VS) fact sheet.* Chapel Hill, NC: University of North Carolina, Frank Porter Graham Child Development Institute, The National Professional Development Center on Autism Spectrum Disorders.

Hume, K., Boyd, B. A., Hamm, J. V., & Kucharczyk, S. (2014). Supporting independence in adolescents on the autism spectrum. *Remedial and Special Education, 35*(2), 102–113.

Hume, K., Loftin, R., & Lantz, J. (2009). Increasing independence in autism spectrum disorders: A review of three focused interventions. *Journal of Autism and Developmental Disorders, 39*(9), 1329–1338.

Hume, K., & Odom, S. (2007). Effects of an individual work system on the independent functioning of students with autism. *Journal of Autism and Developmental Disorders, 37*(6): 1166–1180.

Hume, K., Sreckovic, M., Snyder, K., & Carnahan, C. R. (2014). Smooth transitions: Helping students with autism spectrum disorder navigate the school day. *Teaching Exceptional Children, 47,* 35–45.

Hopko, D. R., Crittendon, J. A., Grant, E., & Wilson, S. A. (2005). The impact of anxiety on performance IQ. *Anxiety, Stress, and Coping, 18*(1), 17–35.

Iadarola, S., Shih, W., Dean, M., Blanch, E., Harwood, R., Hetherington, S., . . . Smith, T. (2018). Implementing a manualized, classroom transition intervention for students with ASD in underresourced schools. *Behavior modification, 42*(1), 126-147.

Individuals with Disabilities Education Act (IDEA) of 1990, PL 101-476, 20 U.S.C. §§ 1400 *et seq.*

Individuals with Disabilities Education Improvement Act (IDEA) of 2004, PL 108-446, 20 U.S.C. §§ 1400 *et seq.*

Iovannone, R., Dunlap, G., Huber, H., & Kincaid, D. (2003). Effective educational practices for students with autism spectrum disorders. *Focus on Autism and Other Developmental Disabilities, 18*(3), 150–165. doi:10.1177/10883576030180030301

Johnson v. Independent School Dist. No. 4 of Bixby, 921 F.2d 1022 (10th Cir. 1990).

Jones, C. R., Simonoff, E., Baird, G., Pickles, A., Marsden, A. J., Tregay, J., . . . Charman, T. (2018). The association between theory of mind, executive function, and the symptoms of autism spectrum disorder. *Autism Research, 11*(1), 95–109.

Joyce, B., & Showers, B. (2002). *Student achievement through staff development: Fundamentals of school renewal* (2nd ed.). White Plains, NY: Longman.

Karsten, A. M., & Carr, J. E. (2009). The effects of differential reinforcement of unprompted responding on the skill acquisition of children with autism. *Journal of Applied Behavior Analysis, 42*(2), 327–334.

Karsten, A. M., Carr, J. E., & Lepper, T. L. (2011). Description of a practitioner model for identifying preferred stimuli with individuals with autism spectrum disorders. *Behavior Modification, 35*, 347–369.

Kellems, R. O., Gabrielsen, T. P., & Williams, C. (2016). Using visual organizers and technology: Supporting executive function, abstract language comprehension, and social learning. In T. Cardon (Ed.), *Technology and the treatment of children with autism spectrum disorder* (pp. 75–86). New York, NY: Springer International Publishing.

Kelly, M. E., & Barnes-Holmes, D. (2015). Measuring implicit and explicit acceptability of reinforcement versus punishment interventions with teachers working in ABA versus mainstream schools. *The Psychological Record, 65*, 251–265.

Knight, V., Sartini, E., & Spriggs, A. D. (2015). Evaluating visual activity schedules as evidence-based practice for individuals with autism spectrum disorders. *Journal of Autism and Developmental Disorders, 45*(1), 157–178.

Koegel, L. K., Park, M. N., & Koegel, R. L. (2014). Using self-management to improve the reciprocal social conversation of children with autism spectrum disorder. *Journal of Autism and Developmental Disorders, 44*(5), 1055–1063.

Kucharczyk, S. (2013). *Reinforcement (R+) fact sheet*. Chapel Hill, NC: University of North Carolina, Frank Porter Graham Child Development Institute, The National Professional Development Center on Autism Spectrum Disorders.

Las Virgenes Unif. Sch. Dist. v. S.K., 54 IDELR 289 (C.D. Cal. 2010).

LB ex rel. KB v. Nebo School Dist., 379 F.3d 966 (10th Cir. 2004).

Ledford, J. R., Lane, J. D., Shepley, C., & Kroll, S. M. (2016). Using teacher-implemented playground interventions to increase engagement, social behaviors, and physical activity for young children with autism. *Focus on Autism and Other Developmental Disabilities, 31*(3), 163–173.

Leithwood, K., Day, C., & Hopkins, D. (2008). Seven strong claims about successful school leadership. *School Leadership and Management, 28*, 27–42.

Lewis, C. (2015). What is improvement science? Do we need it in education? *Educational Researcher, 44*, 54–61.

Louis, K., Leithwood, K., Wahlstrom, K., & Anderson, S. (2010). *Investigating the links to improved learning of learners*. New York, NY: The Wallace Foundation.

Lowrey, K. A., Hollingshead, A., Howery, K., & Bishop, J. B. (2017). More than one way: Stories of UDL, inclusive classrooms, and students with ID. *Research and Practice for Persons with Severe Disabilities*. doi:10.1177/1540796917711668

Maag, J. W. (2001). Rewarded by punishment: Reflections on the disuse of positive reinforcement in schools. *Exceptional Children, 67*, 173–186.

Mancil, G. R., & Pearl, C. E. (2008). Restricted interests as motivators: Improving academic engagement and outcomes of children on the autism spectrum. *Teaching Exceptional Children Plus, 4*(6), 2–15.

Mangin, M. (2007). Facilitating elementary principals' support for instructional teacher leadership. *Educational Administration Quarterly, 43*, 319–357.

Martinez, J. R., Werch, B. L., & Conroy, M. A. (2016). School-based interventions targeting challenging behaviors exhibited by young children with autism spectrum disorder: A systematic literature review. *Education and Training in Autism and Developmental Disabilities, 51*, 265–280.

Mason, R., Kamps, D., Turcotte, A., Cox, S., Feldmiller, S., & Miller, T. (2014). Peer mediation to increase communication and interaction at recess for students with autism spectrum disorders. *Research in Autism Spectrum Disorders, 8*(3), 334–344.

Matson, J. L., & Wilkins, J. (2007). A critical review of assessment targets and methods for social skills excesses and deficits for children with autism spectrum disorders. *Research in Autism Spectrum Disorders, 1*, 28–37.

Mavropoulou, S., Papadopoulou, E., & Kakana, D. (2011). Effects of task organization on the independent play of students with autism spectrum disorders. *Journal of Autism and Developmental Disorders, 41*, 913–925.

Mayton, M. R., Wheeler, J. J., Menendez, A. L., & Zhang, J. (2010). An analysis of evidence-based practices in the education and treatment of learners with autism spectrum disorders. *Education and Training in Autism and Developmental Disabilities, 45*, 539–551.

McCray, E. D., & McHatton, P. A. (2011). Not afraid to have "them" in my classroom: Understanding preservice general educators' perceptions about inclusion. *Teacher Education Quarterly, 38*, 135–155.

McCurdy, E. E., & Cole, C. L. (2014). Use of a peer support intervention for promoting academic engagement of students with autism in general education settings. *Journal of Autism and Developmental Disorders, 44*(4), 883–893.

McLeskey, J., & Waldron, N. (2002). School change and inclusive schools: Lessons learned from practice. *Phi Delta Kappan, 84*, 65–72.

McLeskey, J., & Waldron, N. (2010). Establishing a collaborative school culture through comprehensive reform. *Journal of Educational and Psychological Consultation, 20,* 58–74.

Meadan, H., Ostrosky, M. M., Triplett, B., Michna, A., & Fettig, A. (2011). Using visual supports with young children with autism spectrum disorder. *Teaching Exceptional Children, 43,* 28–35.

Mesibov, G. B., Browder, D. M., & Kirkland, C. (2002). Using individualized schedules as a component of positive behavioral support for students with developmental disabilities. *Journal of Positive Behavior Interventions, 4,* 73–79.

Mesibov, G. B., & Shea, V. (2010). The TEACCH program in the era of evidence-based practice. *Journal of autism and developmental disorders, 40*(5), 570–579.

Mesibov, G., Shea, V., & Schopler, E. (2005). *The TEACCH approach to autism spectrum disorders.* New York, NY: Plenum Press.

Minahan, J., & Rappaport, N. (2012). *The behavior code: A practical guide to understanding and teaching the most challenging students.* Cambridge, MA: Harvard University Press.

Mirenda, P. (2001). Autism, augmentative communication, and assistive technology: What do we really know? *Focus on Autism and Other Developmental Disabilities, 16*(3), 141–152.

Mirenda, P. (2003). Toward functional augmentative and alternative communication for students with autism: Manual signs, graphic symbols, and voice output communication aids. *Language, Speech, and Hearing Services in Schools, 34,* 203–216.

Mirenda, P. (2009). Introduction to AAC for individuals with autism spectrum disorders. In P. Mirenda & T. Iacono (Eds.), *Autism spectrum disorders and AAC* (pp. 3–22). Baltimore, MD: Paul H Brookes Publishing Co.

Morrison, R. S., Sainato, D. M., Benchaaban, D., & Endo, S. (2002). Increasing play skills of children with autism using activity schedules and correspondence training. *Journal of Early Intervention, 25*(1), 58–72.

M.S. v. Fairfax County Sch. Bd., 51 IDELR 148, 553 F.3d 315 (4th Cir. 2009).

Mundy, P., & Mastergeorge, A. (Eds.). (2012). *Educational interventions for students with autism.* John Wiley & Sons.

Mundy, P., Mastergeorge, A. M., & McIntyre, N. S. (2012). Effects of autism on social learning and social attention. In P. Mundy & N. McIntre (Eds.), *Educational interventions for students with autism* (pp. 3–33). San Francisco, CA: John Wiley & Sons.

Mundy, P., & Neal, R. (2001). Neural plasticity, joint attention and a transactional social-orienting model of autism. In L. Glidden (Ed.), *International review of research in mental retardation: Autism* (Vol. 23, pp. 139–168). San Diego, CA: Academic Press.

Mundy, P., Sigman, M., Ungerer, J., & Sherman, T. (1986). Defining the social deficits of autism: The contribution of non-verbal communication measures. *Journal of Child Psychology and Psychiatry and Allied Disciplines, 27,* 657–669.

National Center for Health Statistics. (2013). *Changes in prevalence of parent-reported autism spectrum disorder in school-aged U.S. children: 2007 to 2011–2012.* Hyattsville, MD: S. J. Blumberg.

National Research Council. (2001). *Educating children with autism.* Committee on Educational Interventions for Children with Autism. Washington, DC: National Academies Press.

Neely, L. C., Ganz, J. B., Davis, J. L., Boles, M. B., Hong, E. R., Ninci, J., & Gilliland, W. D. (2016). Generalization and maintenance of functional living skills for individuals with autism spectrum disorder: A review and meta-analysis. *Review Journal of Autism and Developmental Disorders, 3*(1), 37–47.

Neitzel, J. (2008). *Overview of peer-mediated instruction and intervention for children and youth with autism spectrum disorders.* Chapel Hill, NC: University of North Carolina, Frank Porter Graham Child Development Institute, The National Professional Development Center on Autism Spectrum Disorders.

Neitzel, J., & Wolery, M. (2010). Prompting for children and youth with autism spectrum disorders: Online training module. Chapel Hill, NC: National Professional Development Center on Autism Spectrum Disorders, FPG Child Development Institute, UNC-Chapel Hill. No Child Left Behind Act of 2001, PL 107-110, 115 Stat. 1425, 20 U.S.C. § 6301 *et seq.*

Odom, S. L., Cox, A. W., Brock, M. E., & National Professional Development Center on ASD. (2013). Implementation science, professional development, and autism spectrum disorders. *Exceptional Children, 79,* 233–251.

Ohio Center for Autism and Low Incidence (OCALI). Autism Internet Modules. Retrieved from http://www.autisminternetmodules.org. Columbus, OH: OCALI.

O'Reilly, M., Sigafoos, J., Lancioni, G., Edrisinha, C., & Andrews, A. (2005). An examination of the effects of a classroom activity schedule on levels of self-injury and engagement for a child with severe autism. *Journal of Autism and Developmental Disorders, 35*(3), 305–311. doi:10.1007/s10803-005-3294-1

Pazey, B. L., Gevarter, C., Hamrick, J., & Rojeski, L. (2014). Administrator views and knowledge of instructional practices for students with autism spectrum disorders. *Research in Autism Spectrum Disorders, 8,* 1253–1268.

Pierce, J. M., Spriggs, A. D., Gast, D. L., & Luscre, D. (2013). Effects of visual activity schedules on independent classroom transitions for students with autism. International *Journal of Disability, Development and Education, 60,* 253–269.

Porter, N. (2012). Promotion of pretend play for children with high-functioning autism through the use of circumscribed interest. *Early Childhood Education, 40*, 161–167. doi:10.1007/s10643-0120505-1

Pressley, M. (2002). Improving comprehension instruction: A path for the future. In C. C. Block, L. B. Gambrell, & M. Pressley (Eds.), *Improving comprehension instruction: Rethinking research, theory, and classroom practice* (pp. 385–387). San Francisco, CA: Jossey-Bass.

Prizant, B., Wetherby, A., Rubin, E., & Laurent, A. (2003). The SCERTS model, a transactional, family centered approach to enhancing communication and socioemotional abilities of children with autism spectrum disorder. *Infants and Young Children, 16*(4), 296–316.

Quill, K. A. (2017). *Do-watch-listen-say: Social and communication intervention for children with autism* (2nd ed.). Baltimore, MD: Paul H. Brookes Publishing Co.

Randi, J., Newman, T., & Grigorenko, E. (2010). Teaching children with autism to read for meaning: Challenges and possibilities. *Journal of Autism Developmental Disorders, 40*(7), 890–902.

Rehabilitation Act of 1973, 34 C.F.R. Part 104.

Reutebuch, C. K., El Zein, F., & Roberts, G. J. (2015). A systematic review of the effects of choice on academic outcomes for students with autism spectrum disorder. *Research in Autism Spectrum Disorders, 20*, 1–16.

Ricketts, J., Jones, C. R., Happé, F., & Charman, T. (2013). Reading comprehension in autism spectrum disorders: The role of oral language and social functioning. *Journal of Autism and Developmental Disorders, 43*(4), 807–816.

Rowland, C. M. (2009). Presymbolic communicators with autism spectrum disorders. In P. Mirenda & T. Iacono (Eds.), *Autism spectrum disorders and AAC* (pp. 51–82). Baltimore, MD: Paul H. Brookes Publishing Co.

Royer, D. J., Lane, K. L., Cantwell, E. D., & Messenger, M. L. (2017). A systematic review of the evidence base for instructional choice in K–12 settings. *Behavioral Disorders, 42*, 89–107.

Rubin, E. (2017). Use developmental stages to guide treatment in ASD: Considering a child's developmental stage can help SLPs select the best evidence-based treatment. *ASHA Leader, 22*(6), 40–41.

Ruble, L., & McGrew, J. H. (2013). Teacher and child predictors of achieving IEP goals of children with autism. *Journal of Autism and Developmental Disorders, 43*(12), 2748–2763.

Ruble, L. A., & Robson, D. M. (2007). Individual and environmental determinants of engagement in autism. *Journal of Autism and Related Disabilities, 37*, 1457–1468. doi:10.1007/s10803-0060222-y

Salvia, J., Ysseldyke, J., & Bolt, S. (2012). *Assessment: In special and inclusive education*. Belmont, CA: Cengage Learning.

Sam, A., & AFIRM. (2015). *Task analysis*. Chapel Hill, NC: University of North Carolina, National Professional Development Center on Autism Spectrum Disorder, FPG Child Development Center.

Scheuermann, B., & Webber, J. (2002). *Autism: Teaching does make a difference*. Belmont, CA: Wadsworth Publishing Company.

Schreibman, L., Dawson, G., Stahmer, A. C., Landa, R., Rogers, S. J., McGee, G. G., Kasari, C., Ingersoll, B., Kaiser, A.P., Bruinsma, Y., McNerney, E., Wetherby, A., & Halladay, A. (2015). Naturalistic developmental behavioral interventions: Empirically validated treatments for autism spectrum disorder. *Journal of autism and developmental disorders, 45*(8), 2411–2428.

Shuster, B. C., Gustafson, J. R., Jenkins, A. B., Lloyd, B. P., Carter, E. W., & Bernstein, C. F. (2017). Including students with disabilities in positive behavioral interventions and supports: Experiences and perspectives of special educators. *Journal of Positive Behavior Interventions, 19*, 143–157.

Sigafoos, J., O'Reilly, M. F., & Lancioni, G. E. (2009). Functional communication training and choice-making interventions for the treatment of problem behaviors in individuals with autism spectrum disorders. In P. Mirenda & T. Iacono (Eds.), *Autism spectrum disorders and AAC* (pp. 333–354). Baltimore, MD: Paul H. Brookes Publishing Co.

Simpson, R. L. (2005). Evidence-based practices and students with autism spectrum disorders. *Focus on Autism and Other Developmental Disabilities, 20*(3), 140–149.

S.K. v. Parsippany-Troy Hills Bd. of Educ., 51 IDELR 106 (D. N.J. 2008).

Smith, G. J., Schmidt, M. M., Edelen-Smith, P. J., & Cook, B. G. (2013). Pasteur's quadrant as the bridge linking rigor with relevance. *Exceptional Children, 79*, 147–161.

Smith, S. M. (2008). *Visual supports: Online training module*. Columbus, OH: Ohio Center for Autism and Low Incidence.

Solish, A., Perry, A., & Minnes, P. (2010). Participation of children with and without disabilities in social, recreational and leisure activities. *Journal of Applied Research in Intellectual Disabilities, 23*, 226–236.

Steinbrenner, J. R. D., & Watson, L. R. (2015). Student engagement in the classroom: The impact of classroom, teacher, and student factors. *Journal of Autism and Developmental Disorders, 45*(8), 2392–2410.

Stoppelbein, L., Biasini, F., Pennick, M., & Greening, L. (2016). Predicting, internalizing, and externalizing symptoms among children diagnosed with an autism spectrum disorder: The role of routines. *Journal of Child and Family Studies, 25*(1), 251–261.

Storch, E. A., Arnold, E. B., Lewin, A. B., Nadeau, J. M., Jones, A. M., De Nadai, A. S., . . . Murphy, T. K. (2013). The effect of cognitive-behavioral therapy versus treatment as usual for anxiety in children with autism spectrum disorders: A randomized, controlled trial. *Journal of the American Academy of Child & Adolescent Psychiatry, 52*(2), 132–142.

United States Code. Title IX, Education Amendments of 1972. PL 92-318, 86 Stat. 235. (20 U.S.C. § 1681(a).

U.S. Department of Education. (2017a). *Every Student Succeeds Act*. Retrieved from https://www.ed.gov/essa?src=rn

U.S. Department of Education. (2017b). *U.S. Secretary of Education Betsy DeVos announces release of updated ESSA consolidated state plan template*. Retrieved from https://www.ed.gov/news/press-releases/us-secretary-education-betsy-devos-announces-release-updated-essa-consolidated-state-plan-template

Van der Meer, L. A., & Rispoli, M. (2010). Communication interventions involving speech-generating devices for children with autism: A review of the literature. *Developmental Neurorehabilitation, 13*(4), 294–306.

Van der Meer, L., Sigafoos, J., Sutherland, D., McLay, L., Lang, R., Lancioni, G. E., . . . Marschik, P. B. (2014). Preference-enhanced communication intervention and development of social communicative functions in a child with autism spectrum disorder. *Clinical Case Studies, 13*(3), 282–295.

Waldron, N. L., & McLeskey, J. (2010). Establishing a collaborative school culture through comprehensive school reform. *Journal of Educational and Psychological Consultation, 20*(1), 58–74.

The Wallace Foundation. (2013). *The school principal as leader: Guiding schools to better teaching and learning*. New York, NY: The Wallace Foundation.

Watkins, L., O'Reilly, M., Kuhn, M., Gevarter, C., Lancioni, G. E., Sigafoos, J., & Lang, R. (2015). A review of peer-mediated social interaction interventions for students with autism in inclusive settings. *Journal of Autism and Developmental Disorders, 45*(4), 1070–1083.

Wendt, O. (2009). Research on the use of manual signs and graphic symbols in autism spectrum disorders: A systematic review. In P. Mirenda & T. Iacono (Eds.), *Autism spectrum disorders and AAC* (pp. 83–140). Baltimore, MD: Paul H. Brookes Publishing Co.

Wehmeyer, M. L., & Shogren, K. A. (2016). Self-determination and choice. In *Handbook of Evidence-Based Practices in Intellectual and Developmental Disabilities* (pp. 561–584). New York, NY: Springer.

Whalon, K. J., Conroy, M. A., Martinez, J. R., & Werch, B. L. (2015). School-based peer-related social competence interventions for children with autism spectrum disorder: A meta-analysis and descriptive review of single case research design studies. *Journal of Autism and Developmental Disorders, 45*(6), 1513–1531.

Wheatley, M. J. (2002). *Turning to one another: Simple conversations to restore hope to the future*. San Francisco, CA: Berrett-Koshler Publishers.

White, S. W., Koenig, K., & Scahill, L. (2007). Social skills development in children with autism spectrum disorders: A review of the intervention research. *Journal of Autism and Developmental Disorders, 37*(10), 1858–1868.

Whiting, S. W., & Dixon, M. R. (2015). Delayed reinforcement and self-control: Increasing tolerance for delay with children and adults with autism. In F. DiGennaro & D. Reed (Eds.), *Autism service delivery* (pp. 407–435). New York, NY: Springer.

Williams, D. L., Cherkassky, V. L., Mason, R. A., Keller, T. A., Minshew, N. J., & Just, M. A. (2013). Brain function differences in language processing in children and adults with autism. *Autism Research, 6*(4), 288–302.

Wolfberg, P., DeWitt, M., Young, G. S., & Nguyen, T. (2015). Integrated play groups: Promoting symbolic play and social engagement with typical peers in children with ASD across settings. *Journal of Autism and Developmental Disorders, 45*(3), 830–845.

Wong, C., Odom, S. L., Hume, K. A., Cox, A. W., Fettig, A., Kucharczyk, S., . . . Schultz, T. R. (2015). Evidence-based practices for children, youth, and young adults with autism spectrum disorder: A comprehensive review. *Journal of Autism and Developmental Disorders, 45*(7), 1951–1966.

W.S. v. Rye City Sch. Dist., 46 IDELR 285, 454 F. Supp.2d 134 (S.D.N.Y. 2006).

Yell, M.L. (2012). *The law and special education* (3rd ed.). Upper Saddle River, NJ: Pearson/Merrill Education.

Yell, M. L., & Drasgow, E. (2005). *No child left behind: A guide for professionals*. Upper Saddle River, NJ: Pearson/Merrill/Prentice Hall.

Yell, M. L., Drasgow, E., & Lowrey, K. A. (2005). No child left behind and students with autism spectrum disorders. *Focus on Autism and Other Developmental Disabilities, 20*(3), 130–139.

Yell, M., Katsiyannis, A., Ennis, R. P., & Losinski, M. (2013). Avoiding procedural errors in individualized education program development. *Teaching Exceptional Children, 46*(1), 56–64.

Zachary Deal v. Hamilton Bd. of Ed. (6th Cir. 2004, 2008).

Zelazo, P. D., Blair, C. B., & Willoughby, M. T. (2016). *Executive function: Implications for education*. Washington, D.C.: National Center for Education Research. Retrieved from https://ies.ed.gov/ncer/pubs/20172000/pdf/20172000.pdf

Zirkel, P. A. (2002). The autism case law administrative and judicial rulings. *Focus on Autism and Other Developmental Disabilities, 17*(2), 84–93.

Zirkel, P. A. (2011). Autism litigation under the IDEA: A new meaning of "disproportionality." *Journal of Special Education Leadership, 24*(2), 92–110.

Index

Page references followed by *f* or *t* indicate figures or tables, respectively.

academic achievement, 9
academic demands, 10–11
academic standards, 21
access, 84
accommodation plans, 23, 102
achievement, academic, 9
action-oriented strategies, 99
Active Implementation Hub, 81
activity schedules, 41*f*, 56, 59, 60*f*
A.K. v. Alexandria City School Board, 24–25
alternative, incompatible, or other behavior, 31*t*
Americans with Disabilities Act (ADA) of 1990 (PL 101-336), 23, 99
antecedent-based intervention, 31*t*
anxiety, 4, 8–9
Appellant v. Commonwealth of Pennsylvania, Department of Public Welfare, 24
applied behavior analysis (ABA), 24, 81, 99
assessment tools, 85–86
AssistiveWare Core Word, 67
Association for Science in Autism Treatment, 81
attending skills, 24, 99
attention, 7–8, 78, 101
augmentative and alternative communication (AAC) systems, 9, 99
autism, xxii, 2, 7–8, 18
Autism ABA curriculum, 81
Autism Focused Intervention Resources and Modules (AFIRM), 30, 33, 37
Autism Internet Modules, 33, 37, 67, 81
Autism Internet Modules (AIM), 79
Autism Speaks, 12, 33, 37, 81
autism spectrum disorder (ASD), xxii–xxiii, 1–12, 18, 99

Bd. Of Education v. Rowley, 24
behavior, 1–12, 31*t*
behavioral supports, 11, 41*f*, 49–53
    scoring, 53–55, 54*f*–55*f*
Bend Lapine Sch. Dist. v. K.H., 25
best or recommended practices, 1, 30, 99
Brining ABA, 81
Bucks County Department of Mental Health/Mental Retardation, 24

case law, 15–26, 99
CEC (Council for Exceptional Children), xxiii–xxiv, 36, 100
CEEDAR Evidence-Based Practices for Students With Severe Disabilities, 37
Centers for Disease Control and Prevention (CDC), 12
change models, 74
Child Find, 16, 100
choices, student
    determining, 51–52
    offering and honoring, 41*f*, 52–53, 54*f*, 55
Civil Rights Act of 1964 (PL 88-352), 23
classroom activities, 41*f*, 62*f*, 67
classroom areas or spaces, 41*f*, 44–45, 45*f*, 62*f*
classroom checklist, 83–98
classroom materials, 41*f*, 43–44, 45*f*, 46
classroom observation tool (COT), *See* Evidence-Based Practice Classroom Observation Tool (EBP COT)
classroom schedules, 41*f*, 46
Closer Look, 33
coaches, 80
cognitive theory, 2–7
coherence, central, 2, 5–7
collaboration, xxiii, xxiv, 100
Collaboration Guide, 76, 77*f*
collaborative professional development, 79–80
collaborative school cultures, 71–82
communication considerations, 9, 41*f*, 63–67
    for effective leaders, 76–78
    scoring, 65–67, 66*f*–67*f*
    social-communication, 102
communication devices, 65
communication instruction, 41*f*, 64, 66*f*

Communication Matrix, 63, 68
communication systems, 41*f*, 63–65, 66*f*
complaint resolution, 20–21
confidence, 84
conflict resolution, 76
consent, 20
Corpus Christi Indep. Sch. Dist. v. Christopher N., 25
Council for Exceptional Children (CEC), xxiii–xxiv, 36, 100
County School Board of Henrico County VA v. R. T. et al., 24
culture, school, 71–82, 102

data collection, 41*f*, 62*f*, 78
Deal, Zachary, 24
developing practices, 30
developmental delay, 18, 100
differential reinforcement, 31*t*
direction, 72–73, 75
disability, 23
discipline, 78
discrete trial teaching or training, 31*t*, 34, 100
disposition, 76–78
distributed leadership, 78, 100
diversity of thought, 76
due process hearing, 20–21, 100

echolalia, 102
Education Amendments of 1972 (PL 92-318), 23
educational programs, 10–11, 73–74
efficacy, 29, 100
E.G. v. City School District of New Rochelle, 25
Elementary and Secondary Education Act of 1965 (PL 89-10), 21–22
emotional management, 11
Endrew v. Douglas County School District, 25
engagement, 10
environmental considerations, 41*f*, 42–55, 45*f*
environmental supports, 41*f*, 57
    scoring, 59, 61*f*
errors, procedural, 102
errors, substantive, 103
evaluation, 17, 20, 101
Every Student Succeeds Act (ESSA) of 2015 (PL 114-95), 21–22, 100
evidence, practice-based, 101
evidence-based practice(s), xxii, xxiii, 29–31, 86, 87*t*
    characteristics of, 34–36
    definition of, 29–30, 72, 100
    implementation of, 33–34, 84–86
    requirements for, 103
    resources for, 37, 79
    strategies for developing and sustaining, 74–80
    for students with ASD, 31*t*–32*t*, 31–34
Evidence-Based Practice Classroom Checklist (EBP CC), 86–96, 90*f*, 94*t*
Evidence-Based Practice Classroom Observation Tool (EBP COT), xiii, xvii, 35, 39–68, 41*f*
    case example, 35–36
    communication considerations, 41*f*, 63–67, 66*f*–67*f*
    environmental considerations, 41*f*, 42–55, 45*f*
    instructional considerations, 41*f*, 55–63, 60*f*–62*f*
    scoring, 40–42, 59–63, 60*f*–62*f*, 65–67, 66*f*–67*f*
executive function (EF), 2–4, 100
explosive behavior, 9–10
extended school year (ESY) services, 25, 100

faculty, 72–73
feelings, 9
fidelity, 34, 100
free appropriate public education (FAPE), 16, 18–20, 24–25, 100

graphic organizers, 6, 101
group work
    instructional configurations, 32*t*, 41*f*, 43–46, 45*f*, 59, 60*f*
    student-directed, 67

hearings, due process, 20–21, 100
home base, 53

implementation drivers, 74, 101
improvement science, 72–74, 101
independence, 41*f*, 58–59
individualized education programs (IEPs), 17–19, 101
    case law related to, 24–25
    procedural errors, 19, 102
    substantive errors, 19, 103
individualized schedules, 48, 49*f*
Individuals with Disabilities Education Act (IDEA) of 2004 (PL 108-446), xxii, 16–21, 83, 101
innovation science, 74, 101
instruction
    communication, 41*f*, 64, 66*f*
    management of, 73–74
    objectives of, 41*f*, 56–59
    social skills, 41*f*, 65, 66*f*
    systematic, 10, 41*f*, 48, 49*f*, 57–59, 61*f*–62*f*
instructional activities, 41*f*, 62*f*, 67
instructional considerations, 41*f*, 55–63
    scoring, 59–63, 60*f*–62*f*
instructional format, 41*f*, 55–56
    varied configurations, 41*f*, 43–46, 45*f*, 59, 60*f*
instructional materials, *See* classroom materials

Johnson v. Independent School, 25
joint attention, 7, 101

Las Virgenes Unif. Sch. Dist. v. S.K., 25
laws and legislation, xxii, 15–26
L.B. and J.B. on Behalf of K.B. v. Nebo Sch. Dist. et al., 24
leadership, xxii, xxiv–xxv
    for change, 72–74
    for collaborative school culture, 71–82
    distributed or shared, 78, 100
    for improving factuly and staff performance, 72–74

learning, 1–12
least restrictive environment (LRE), xxii, 16, 20, 25, 101
legislation, 15–26, 101
life skills, 58
LRP Education Administration and Law (web site), 25

major life activity, 23, 101
mediation, 20–21, 101
modeling, video, 8, 32t, 103
monitoring progress, 34, 58, 102
M.S. Ex. Rel. Simchick v. Fairfax County Sch. Bd., 25
multidisciplinary evaluation, 17
multidisciplinary teams, 17
multifactored approach, 25

narratives, social, 32t
National Autism Association, 33, 37
National Autism Center (NAC), xxiii–xxiv, 12, 30–33, 37
    evidence-based practices, 31, 86, 87t
    National Standards Project, 30, 84
National Center on Universal Design for Learning, 68
National Professional Development Center (NPDC), xxiii, 30, 37, 81
    Autism Focused Intervention Resources and Modules (AFIRM), 30, 33, 37
    evidence-based practices, 31, 86, 87t
    practice guides, 79
National Professional Development Center on Autism Spectrum Disorders (NPDC on ASD), 68, 84
National Standards Project, 30, 84
naturalistic interventions, 32t, 34, 101
naturalistic settings, 58
No Child Left Behind (NCLB) Act of 2001 (PL 107-110), 21–22, 83
notetaking, structured, 50, 51f
notice, 20

observation tool, *See* Evidence-Based Practice Classroom Observation Tool (EBP COT)
Ohio Center for Autism and Low Incidence, 81
Ohio Center for Low Incidence Disabilities, 37
organization for change, 75
other health impaired, 18, 101

parents, 17, 32t
Partington Behavior Analysts, 81
pedagogy, 34, 101
peer communication, 64–65, 67f
peer-reviewed research, 19, 101
PEERS (Program for the Education and Enrichment of Relationship Skills), 68
personnel, 75, 80
physical organization, 41f, 42–46, 45f
Picture Exchange Communication System, 32t
placement, 24–25
plan-do-study-act (PDSA) cycles, 78–79
positive behavior interventions and supports (PBIS), 50–52

positive behavior skills, 11
practice-based evidence, 101
practice guides, 79
practice opportunities, 58
preservice professionals, xxv
priming, 6, 102
prior written notice, 20, 102
problem solving, 76
procedural errors, 19, 102
procedural safeguards, 16, 20–21, 102
professional development, xxv, 37, 79–80
professional standards, 36
Program for the Education and Enrichment of Relationship Skills (PEERS), 68
progress monitoring, 34, 102
Project Core, 68
promising practices, 30, 102
prompts and prompting, 32t, 57
    scoring, 59–63, 61f–62f

recommended practices, 30, 99
recoupment, 102
reculturing, 102
reflection, 80
regression, 25, 102
regulations, 15–26, 102
Rehabilitation Act of 1973 (PL 93-112), 102
    Section 504, 17, 23, 102
reinforcement, 31, 32t, 41f, 50–52, 54f, 102
    individualized, 52, 55
related services, 102
repetitive behavior, 2
research, 72–74
    future directions, 95–96
    peer-reviewed, 19, 101
research-based practices, 30, 102
resources, 12, 25–26, 33, 37, 67–68, 81
response interruption/redirection, 32t
restricted interests, 2
routines, 10

safeguards, 76, 102
SCERTS, 12
schedules
    activity, 56, 59, 60f
    classroom, 41f, 46
    scoring, 46, 47f, 48–49, 49f, 59, 60f
    staff, 41f, 47f
    student, 41f, 46–49, 49f
    visual, 8, 41f, 46–49, 47f, 49f, 103
school change models, 74
school culture, 71–82, 102
school reform research, 72–74
scripted language, 32t, 102
Section 504 accommodation plans, 23, 102
self-regulation, 9, 11, 32t, 102
shared attention, 101
shared leadership, 78
S.K. v. Parsippany-Troy Hills Bd. of Educ., 25
social attention, 7–8

social-communication, 1, 102
social demands, 10–11
social skills instruction, 41f, 65, 66f
social transaction theory, 2
special education services, 16–18, 20–21
special education teachers, 36
staff behavior, 41f, 58–59, 67, 73
    communication considerations, 64, 66f
    scoring, 62f, 63
staff schedules, 41f, 47f
standardized benchmark assessment tool, 83–98
standards, 21, 103
STAR method, 80, 103
state complaint resolution process, 20–21, 103
state educational agency (SEA), 21, 103
stereotyped movements, 18, 103
stress management, 8–9, 76
structured notetaking, 50, 51f
student choices
    determining, 51–52
    offering and honoring, 41f, 52–53, 54f, 55
student schedules, 41f, 46–49, 49f
students with ASD, xxii–xxiii, 1–12, 18
substantive errors, 19, 103
systematic instruction, 10, 41f, 48, 49f, 57–58
    scoring, 59, 61f–62f
systemic implementation of EBP, 85
systems organization, 75

task analysis, 6, 32t, 103
teaching, 73–74
    discrete trial, 31t, 34, 100
    professional development resources for, 37
    professional standards for, 36
terminology, 30
theory of mind (ToM), 2, 4–5, 103
time delay, 32t, 34, 103
time management, 84–85
ToM, *See* theory of mind

transactional social attentional model, 7–8
transition(s), 41f, 54f, 55
transition statements, 19, 103
transition supports, 41f, 53, 55, 55f
Treatment and Education of Autistic and related Communication Handicapped Children (TEACCH), 24

United States Supreme Court, 25
Universal Design for Learning (UDL), 40–42
Universal Design for Learning Implementation and Research Network, 68
U.S. Department of Education
    IDEA resources, 19–20, 26
    NCLB question-and-answer resource, 22, 26
    Office of Special Education Programs, 20
    Section 504 accommodation plans question-and-answer guide, 23

video modeling, 8, 32t, 103
video resources, 81
vision, 72–73, 75
visual schedules, 8, 41f, 46–49, 103
    scoring, 46, 47f, 48–49, 49f
visual supports, 3–4, 32t, 41f, 50, 58, 103
    examples, 50, 51f
    scoring, 54f, 55

weak central coherence (WCC), 2, 5–7
web sites, 12, 25–26, 37, 67–68
work systems, 41f, 56–57, 59, 60f–61f
Wrightslaw (web resource), 26
written notice, prior, 20, 102
W.S. v. Rye City Sch. Dist., 25

Zachary Deal v. Hamilton Bd. of Ed., 24
zero reject, 16, 103